ENDING AFFIRMATIVE ACTION

Ending AFFIRMATIVE ACTION

THE CASE FOR COLORBLIND JUSTICE

TERRY EASTLAND

BasicBooks
A Division of HarperCollins*Publishers*

Copyright © 1996, 1997 by Terry Eastland.
Published by BasicBooks,
A Division of HarperCollins Publishers, Inc.

Designed by Elliott Beard

Library of Congress Cataloging-in-Publication Data

Eastland, Terry.
    Ending affirmative action : the case for colorblind justice / by
Terry Eastland.
        p.   cm.
    Includes bibliographical references and index.
    ISBN 0-465-01388-0 (cloth)
    ISBN 0-465-01389-9 (paper)
    1. Affirmative action programs—United States. I. Title.
HF5549.5.A34E25   1996
    331.13'3'0973—dc20   96-11276

97 98 99 00 ❖/RRD 9 8 7 6 5 4 3 2 1

For Jill and Katie

We all want progress, but if you're on the wrong road, progress means doing an about-turn and walking back to the right road; in that case, the man who turns back soonest is the most progressive.

—*C. S. Lewis*

Contents

1

By Any Other Name

When he joined the police department in Memphis, Tennessee, in 1975, Danny O'Connor wanted someday to make sergeant. In 1988, he took a shot at it. Like the other 209 officers competing for 75 promotions, O'Connor completed the written exam and sat for his interview. When his scores on both parts were added to points awarded for seniority and on-the-job performance over the past year, he placed fifty-sixth on the Composite Scores List. The department had indicated that the 75 top-ranked officers on this list would be the ones promoted. O'Connor knew his ranking and thought he had realized his dream. But then affirmative action struck.

When the candidates took the written exam, they were required on the answer sheets to indicate their race and sex. On the basis of this information, the department created a second set of rankings—the Promotional Eligibility List. This new list, created to satisfy the department's affirmative action plan, modified the Composite Scores List by bumping blacks up into every third position. Necessarily, whoever had been there originally was bumped down. Some 26 blacks were on the eligibility list; 7 had been on the composite list. So 19 blacks (originally ranked between 76 and 132) had been bumped up the list—in some cases way up—and were promoted. Whites were bumped down, and those who had been ranked in the lower regions of the composite list were bumped below the seventy-fifth spot—and thus out of a promotion. Danny O'Connor, who is white, was one of these.

Undaunted, O'Connor tried again the next year. The department proceeded much as it had in 1988, using the same four-part process (though it changed the basis for awarding seniority points). Of 177 candidates, 94 would be promoted. They received their composite scores and on the basis of those scores were ranked. Affirmative action stepped in again, however, as the department used race to rerank the candidates. Where 15 blacks had made the top 94 on the composite list, 33 blacks were among the top 94 on the new list. Eighteen blacks had been bumped up into the top 94, and 18 whites previously in the top 94 had been bumped down. One of these was O'Connor, seventy-fifth on the original list.

Over the two years, while Danny O'Connor remained a patrol officer, 43 candidates with lower composite scores were bumped ahead of him and promoted to sergeant in the name of affirmative action.

Affirmative action was begun in the late 1960s to benefit blacks and over time has come to embrace certain other minority groups, as well as women (in the areas of employment and public contracting). There are, of course, forms of affirmative action that do not bump people out of an opportunity on account of race or sex. In employment, these forms of affirmative action can include outreach, recruitment, and training programs that are open to all, regardless of race or sex. But the affirmative action Danny O'Connor experienced is the kind that for years has been unsettling America. While it takes different guises and has different justifications, this type of affirmative action makes a virtue of race, ethnicity, and sex in order to determine who gets an opportunity and who does not. To call it by its proper name, it is discrimination.

Cheryl Hopwood had an experience like Danny O'Connor's. In 1992 she applied for admission to the University of Texas School of Law. She had earned a degree in accounting from California State University in 1988, achieving a 3.8 grade point average and scoring 39 (the highest score being 48) on the Law School Admissions Test (LSAT). She was, in addition, a certified public accountant. In the four years since finishing at Cal State, Hopwood had married and moved close to San Antonio, where her husband, an Air Force captain, was stationed. A Texas resident, she had just given birth to her first child when she applied for admission to the prestigious University of Texas law school.

Hopwood thought her credentials were excellent, but the law school turned her down. "The only thing I could think of," she says of her initial response to the news, "was that the class the school admitted must have been very, very good." Wanting to find out just how good, she discovered instead that because she is white she had not been able to compete with all other applicants for admission. Under the school's affirmative action plan, 15 percent of the approximately 500 seats in the class had been set aside for blacks and Mexican-Americans, who were admitted under academic standards different from — in fact, lower than — those for all other students. Hopwood's admissions score — a composite number based on her undergraduate grade point average and her LSAT score—was 199. Eleven resident Mexican-American applicants had scores this high or higher, and only one resident black had a score of 199. The school admitted all twelve of these applicants but not Hopwood, and then, in pursuit of its 15 percent affirmative action goal, admitted 84 additional resident Mexican-American and black applicants. Their scores were lower—in some cases substantially lower—than Hopwood's. Indeed, the school admitted every resident black with a score of 185 or higher. If Hopwood were black or Mexican-American, she would have been admitted.

Hopwood's experience differs from O'Connor's only in terms of the opportunity she sought, an educational one. Like O'Connor, she was bumped down and out by affirmative action that bumped others below her up and in. "I can't change my race," she says.

Neither can Randy Pech. The owner of Adarand Constructors, Inc., in Colorado Springs, Colorado, Pech, who is white, submitted the low bid for the guardrail portion on a federal highway construction project. But the business went to Gonzales Construction Company, which submitted a higher bid but is Hispanic-owned. That happens to be a virtue in the eyes of the U.S. Department of Transportation, which enforces a law that "sets aside" a portion of federal construction funds for businesses owned by minorities and women. Pech says he competes with four other companies in Colorado that build guardrails. Two are owned by Hispanics. Two are owned by women. Set-aside laws, he says, work solely against him. "If I weren't here, they'd have no impact."

Jerry Henry learned about set-asides at a university. Henry owns a painting company in Columbus, Ohio, and for years had bid on jobs at Ohio State University, the source of about 20 percent of his business, by his estimate. One day in the spring of 1983, he recalls, he was at the university's Decorating Department, where "I was told that there was a bid coming up but that it was only for minority bidders." Henry, who is white, discovered that under a relatively new state law—the Ohio Minority Business Enterprise Act of 1980—some 15 percent of the work the state contracts out to the private sector was reserved for minority-owned firms. "We were still invited to bid on some projects," he says, but the situation worsened. "By late 1985, I was totally shut off from the Decorating Department." And by 1989, the Residence and Dining Halls Department also dried up as a source of business. The university decided that to meet the 15 percent goal for all of its contracting, it would have to set aside 100 percent of the painting jobs for minority bidders.

Unlike Randy Pech, Henry did not simply lose business because a minority contractor with a higher bid than his got the job instead. Rather, he was barred altogether from bidding on painting projects at Ohio State. Because of his race, he was not even allowed to compete.

Sharon Taxman knows what it is like to be an explicit target of affirmative action. In the late 1980s, the Board of Education of Piscataway Township in New Jersey faced a decline in the number of students choosing business education courses at Piscataway High School. In the spring of 1989, the board decided to lay off one of the school's ten business education teachers. The decision came down to a choice between laying off Taxman, who is white, and Debra Williams, who is black. Invoking its affirmative action plan, which prefers blacks and other minorities over whites, the board chose to retain Williams. The board used its affirmative action plan as skillfully as a surgeon does a scalpel, removing Taxman, the white person.

Danny O'Connor, Cheryl Hopwood, Randy Pech, Jerry

Henry, and Sharon Taxman decided to challenge in court the discrimination that goes by the name of affirmative action.[1] They are gallant foot soldiers in the fight against a policy that by allocating opportunity on the basis of race and sex is dividing and damaging the nation. The time has come for us to end it.

A Bargain with the Devil

More than half a century ago, during World War II, our government unjustly assumed disloyalty on the part of all Japanese-Americans on the West Coast. They were evacuated and forced to live in camps resembling prisons. The Supreme Court upheld as a wartime emergency the government's racially discriminatory action in two cases decided in 1943 and 1944.

Nonetheless, the opinions by the justices made clear that they understood the moral principle at stake. Indeed, one could say that the Court made its decisions even though its members knew better. Specifically, they knew, as the Court's opinion in the first of the two cases declared, that "distinctions between citizens solely because of their ancestry are by their very nature odious to a free people whose institutions are founded upon the doctrine of equality."[2]

The civil rights movement, then battling against segregation in the South and border states, agreed. The movement's lawyers knew that racial distinctions invariably lead to racial discrimination and its constant behavioral symptom: different treatment on account of race. These lawyers began arguing for law that would deny government the ability to distinguish and discriminate on the basis of race—colorblind law, as it was called. In the 1950s, the political leaders of the civil rights movement took their moral case to the nation, arguing from colorblind principle that each person should be treated as an individual, without regard to race. The principle was vindicated when Congress passed the landmark Civil Rights Act of 1964, which comprehensively outlawed racial discrimination. Congress understood "discrimination" to mean, in the words of Senator Hubert Humphrey, "a distinction in treatment given to different individuals because of their different race."[3] But colorblind law and colorblind principle were soon made to yield to affirmative action.

The original purpose of affirmative action was to remedy the ill effects of past discrimination against blacks. "To get beyond racism," as Justice Harry Blackmun famously put it in his opinion in the 1978 case *Regents of the University of California* v. *Bakke,* "we must first take account of race."[4] "Taking account of race" meant distinguishing on the basis of race and treating blacks differently. In the old days, this would have looked like racial discrimination. But the first advocates of affirmative action assured us that affirmative action was well intentioned. Race could be regulated to good effect, we were told, and affirmative action would end soon enough, with the nation the better for it. As one of the early architects of affirmative action put it, "We are in control of our own history."[5]

By the early 1970s, affirmative action was extended to cover additional minority groups and in some contexts women, and over the years its backers have offered additional justifications, such as overcoming "underrepresentation" and achieving "diversity." But the nation has paid a steep price for departing from colorblind principle, for affirmative action has turned out to be a bargain with the devil. Not only has the policy worked discrimination against those it does not favor— a Danny O'Connor or a Cheryl Hopwood, for example—but it also has guaranteed the salience of race and ethnicity in the life of the nation, thus making it harder to overcome the very tendency the civil rights movement once condemned: that of regarding and judging people in terms of their racial and ethnic groups.

To state the obvious: affirmative action makes race and ethnicity salient by naming the minority groups it ostensibly benefits. The affirmative action that the police officer Danny O'Connor encountered targeted blacks. The Texas law school applicant Cheryl Hopwood experienced a plan that drew a circle around blacks and Mexican-Americans. The affirmative action plan employed against the Piscataway high school teacher Sharon Taxman encompassed blacks, Hispanics, Asian-Americans, and American Indians. The same groups were included in the Ohio Minority Business Enterprise Act, which cut Jerry Henry out of competition for painting business. Randy Pech, the owner of Adarand Constructors, lost the job on which he was the low bidder to a business owned by Hispanics, one of the minority groups preferred by the U.S. Transportation Department's affirmative action scheme (others are blacks, American Indians, and Asian-Pacific Americans). The Small Business Administration (SBA), which keeps the federal government's list of racial and ethnic groups targeted for set-asides at Transportation and other agencies, spelled out almost two decades ago the subgroups within the Asian-Pacific American classification: persons with roots in Japan, China, the Philippines, Vietnam, Korea, Samoa, Guam, the U.S. Trust Territory of the Pacific, the Northern Marianas, Laos, Cambodia, and Taiwan. In the 1980s, the SBA accepted petitions from Sri Lankans, Tongans, Asian-Indians, and Indonesians to be included on its affirmative action roster.[6]

By formally drawing racial and ethnic lines, affirmative action invites judgments about the abilities and achievements of those who are members of the targeted groups. One persistent judgment is that those who received a benefit through affirmative action could not have secured it on their own. In many cases, this happens to be true. Indeed, the whole point of many affirmative action programs is to help those who otherwise could not have landed the opportunity in open competition. The program Cheryl Hopwood encountered at the Texas law school lowered the school's academic standards in order to admit blacks and Mexican-Americans. The school also segregated the applications of blacks and Mexican-Americans, assigning them to a separate admissions committee while a different committee reviewed the merits of the "white and other" applicants. Thus treated differently, the members of the two minority groups competed only among themselves. Had they competed among all applicants under the same standards, many fewer blacks and Mexican-Americans would have gained admission to the Texas law school.

This is not, however, the whole story. The black and Mexican-American applicants admitted under affirmative action were not *un*qualified to study law; their academic qualifications were good enough to win admission under non–affirmative action standards at fully two-thirds of the nation's law schools.[7] Affirmative action thus stigmatizes beneficiaries who could succeed—and be seen to succeed—without it. At the same time, it stigmatizes those eligible for it who are not its beneficiaries. At the Texas law school, one Hispanic student who had a composite score good enough to warrant admission under the standards applicable to "whites and others" said that he felt he needed a shirt indicating he got in on his own, just to let people know the genuine nature of his accomplishment.[8] It is sadly ironic that affirmative action can put a non–affirmative action minority student in this situation, but the student's response is hardly irrational. He knows that the mere existence of the law school's program invites people to think, in his case: "You're Hispanic, so you got in through affirmative action."

An abiding truth about much affirmative action is that those who are its ostensible beneficiaries are burdened with the task of overcoming it—if, that is, they wish to be treated as individuals, without regard to race. It is possible, of course, for someone extended an opportunity through affirmative action to overcome it by doing extraordinarily well, meeting the highest standards. But some minorities have concluded that the best way to escape the public implications of affirmative action is to say "no" when they know it is being offered. In 1983, Freddie Hernandez, a Hispanic who serves in the Miami fire department, rejected an affirmative action promotion to lieutenant. Instead, he waited three years until he had the necessary seniority and had scored high enough to qualify for the promotion under procedures that applied to nonminorities. This decision cost Hernandez $4,500 a year in extra pay and forced him to study 900 additional hours to attain the required test results. But, as he proudly told the *Wall Street Journal*, "I knew I could make it on my own."[9]

Hernandez rejected the affirmative action bargain. He wanted to be judged as an individual, on his own merits, without regard to his ethnic background—just the way the old civil rights pioneers said he had a right to be judged.

The Language of Affirmative Action

Affirmative action has taken a toll on public discourse. Through the years its supporters have said, for example, that they do not support quotas. But painter Jerry Henry experienced a 100 percent quota at Ohio State. And there was a reason police officer Danny O'Connor was bumped down and out of a promotion. There was a reason black officers were bumped up into every third position. The Memphis police department was trying to fill a quota that reserved one-third of the promotions for blacks. Bumping blacks up into every third position on the list of 75 may have been a crude way of making the quota, but it got the job done. Faced with evidence of a quota, supporters of affirmative action backtrack, saying that they are against "hard and fast" or "rigid" quotas and for "flexible" goals. The distinction in practice may mean that a slightly lesser number of the preferred minority group or women is hired or admitted. This happened at the University of Texas School of Law, which in 1992 fell a bit short of its 15 percent goal for black and Mexican-American admittees. But whatever term is used to describe what the law school was doing, race was determining the bulk of these admissions decisions.

Affirmative action supporters may concede that race is the determining factor but insist that the practice benefits only qualified people. Yet what matters to those competing for a limited number of openings or opportunities is not whether they are qualified in the abstract, but whether they are *more* qualified than the others seeking that position. The rankings Danny O'Connor earned showed that he was more qualified than officers bumped above him and promoted to sergeant on account of race. And Cheryl Hopwood's composite score showed she was more qualified than many of those with lower scores who were admitted under the Texas law school's affirmative action plan. Some supporters of affirmative action respond by claiming that differences in qualifications—above a certain minimum—are negligible. They will not say, however, that differences in qualifications are unimportant in the case of those who are *not* eligible for affirmative action. And judgments about who is better are routinely made by all of us when we seek the services of, say, a doctor or lawyer. Not surprisingly, though most unfortunately, some affirmative action programs have dispensed with even minimal qualifications. In 1993, in an effort to increase the "diversity" of its workforce, the U.S. Forest Service's Pacific Southwest Region established "upward mobility positions" that it set aside for applicants who do not meet the service's usual employment requirements. The dictionary of affirmative action does not appear to include words like "excellence" and "outstanding" and "best."

Supporters of affirmative action do have a word they use often: "voluntary," as in "Most affirmative action is voluntary." The common meaning of "voluntary" is that which is done without compulsion or obligation, freely, even spontaneously. But the truth is that much of what is called voluntary affirmative action is in effect compelled by government or its agencies and institutions. Consider, for example, the Labor Department's enforcement of a 1965 executive order requiring nondiscrimination and affirmative action on the part of federal contractors, who employ roughly a third of the nation's workforce. The purpose of the Labor Department program is not to root out proven discrimination but to overcome "underutilization," defined in complex terms involving a variety of demographic considerations. Basically, if the numbers of minorities and women "utilized" by a federal contractor are below their "availability," as the Labor Department calculates it, then the contractor must correct this "underutilization" through hiring and promotion "goals and timetables." If the contractor does not take the necessary affirmative action, it could lose the federal contract. That seldom happens, of course, because contractors "voluntarily" do the government's bidding.

Government has other means of encouraging "voluntary" affirmative action, such as an offer of money. There was such an offer in the case involving Randy Pech. The guardrail job he sought was part of a larger highway construction project in the San Juan National Forest that the Transportation Department had awarded to a company named Mountain Gravel and Construction Company. Gonzales Construction was awarded the guardrail job even though Pech submitted the low bid because of something called the "Subcontracting Compensation Clause"—a term that conceals its true meaning. The Transportation Department uses this clause to induce prime contractors on federally funded highway construction projects to subcontract work to businesses owned by minorities or women, even if their bid is not the low one. The reason the department uses the clause is to help meet congressional demands that 10 percent of the monies appropriated for transportation construction projects be awarded to minority- and female-owned businesses. The ostensible theory of the Subcontracting Compensation Clause is that the prime contractor needs to be "compensated" for the higher costs incurred in helping minorities and women, who are going to charge more for the jobs they do. The clause is a carrot: if the prime contractor awards jobs to minorities or women, then the Transportation Department pays the prime contractor a bonus of 10 percent of the dollar amount of the subcontracts. The job awarded to Gonzales Construction amounted to slightly more than $100,000. So, for practicing affirmative action—and committing racial discrimination— Mountain Gravel pocketed a $10,000 bonus, paid by taxpayers. There is a Subcontracting Compensation Clause in most federal agency contracts. In its absence, firms like Mountain Gravel would follow the standard race- and sex-blind rule under which the low bidder wins the subcontracting business.

The term "affirmative action" itself merits notice. Those bumped aside by affirmative action know what kind of term it is. They know it is a euphemism. When the Piscataway board of education laid off Sharon Taxman, she got the news in a letter from the board's director of personnel, who explained: "The board of education has decided on its commitment to affirmative action as a means of breaking the tie in seniority entitlement."[10] The blunt truth, of course, was that because Williams is black and Taxman is white, Taxman had to be laid off.

The Myth of "Temporary" Affirmative Action

In the late 1960s and during the 1970s, advocates of affirmative action often said that it was only a temporary measure whose success would render it unnecessary in the future. But these temporary measures often seem to go on and on and on—well beyond the point at which they were supposed to end.

Let us return to Danny O'Connor's story. It actually began back in 1974, when the Justice Department sued the city of Memphis under Title VII of the Civil Rights Act of 1964, alleging that it had engaged in unlawful employment discrimination against blacks and women. Quickly, the city and the federal government settled the suit through a consent decree that won federal court approval. Other lawsuits followed: black police officers sued the city in 1975, charging racially discriminatory promotion practices, and a black firefighter filed a similar suit in 1977. Judicially approved consent decrees also concluded these cases. And then, in 1981, the city and the federal government amended their 1974 agreement. Though the city never admitted to past discrimination, it did agree to hire and promote blacks and females in proportions, as the 1981 decree put it, "approximating their respective proportions in the relevant Shelby County civilian labor force."

Now, we may regard the lawsuits of the 1970s as necessary in forcing change upon an Old South city. And for the sake of argument, let us concede that proportional hiring and promoting were needed to effect change in the 1970s and early 1980s. But having achieved proportional representation in the fire and police workforces by the mid-1980s, the city did not end its attachment to proportionalism, as Danny O'Connor's case shows. City officials claim that the 1981 decree tied their hands, but it did not *require* race-based employment decisions. In fact, the decree provided that the city was not obligated to hire or promote a less-qualified person over a better-qualified person. The inconvenient truth appears to be that proportional hiring and promoting proved administratively a lot easier for the city than trying to treat applicants and employees fairly without regard to race. In 1994, a federal appeals court rejected the city's motion to dismiss the complaint brought by Danny O'Connor and other white employees. In its opinion the court expressed concern that the city "has made no effort to limit the duration of [the race-based promotional] remedies."[11]

The federal executive branch has made no effort in this regard, either. The 1981 consent decree governing the city of Memphis could have been dissolved by agreement of the parties as early as March 1984, but the Justice Department under Ronald Reagan did not ask the city to end its hiring and promotional remedies. Nor, for that matter, did the Justice

Department under George Bush. And when the city found itself in 1994 in the court of appeals trying to fend off Danny O'Connor's lawsuit, the Justice Department under Bill Clinton filed a brief in support of the city's never-ending affirmative action.

The story of affirmative action without end is found outside the Old South and in programs adopted by elective branches of government. When the Ohio legislature passed the Minority Business Enterprise Act in 1980, it did not determine whether the state had engaged in past discrimination against minority contractors or minorities in general. Failing to ground the set-aside in a rationale that at least in theory might have confined the life of the program, the legislature declared that the purpose of the legislation was to promote "the general welfare of the people." The statute placed no limits at all on its lifetime.

The prospect of unending affirmative action has become all too real in recent years with the discovery of the "diversity" rationale. Consider again the Piscataway story. The Piscataway board of education did not justify its decision to lay off Sharon Taxman in terms of affirmative action necessary to remedy past discrimination—there had been no discrimination—or to overcome a minority imbalance in its workforce generally, for there was no such imbalance. Instead, Piscataway justified its decision in terms of ensuring faculty diversity—making sure that minorities were in effect proportionally represented even in a very small teaching unit, in this case the high school's ten-person business education department. It is impossible to see how the board could ever retire an affirmative action plan premised on this idea, because teachers retire or resign not according to diversity but according to other factors, usually personal ones. So the prospect of an inadequately diverse teaching unit always will have to be anticipated, and therefore affirmative action will always be necessary to preserve the school board's understanding of diversity at any given moment, though at the expense of individual rights.

The Choice

Failing to make good on its promise to be only temporary, affirmative action has entrenched itself more deeply in our institutions, attracting political constituencies that demand its retention. Surveys of public opinion show, however, that preferences have never enjoyed the majority support of the American people. Moreover, the substantial immigration the nation has experienced since, coincidentally, the advent of affirmative action is rendering the policy increasingly incoherent.

Roughly three-quarters of those who come to the United States each year are of a race or ethnic background that makes them eligible for affirmative action, and most affirmative action programs are indifferent as to whether their beneficiaries are U.S. citizens or not, or whether, if they are U.S. citizens, they recently arrived here or not. We thus have a policy originally designed to remedy the ill effects of past discrimination that is open to immigrants with no past in the United States during which they could have experienced discrimination.

The incoherence of such affirmative action is perhaps best demonstrated in Florida, where the wealthy Fanjul family live. The Fanjuls, who have kept their Cuban citizenship in order to avoid paying U.S. estate taxes, have taken advantage of their "minority" status to win government contracts set aside for Hispanics. The finance director of Broward County, Florida, told *Forbes* magazine that it was "irrelevant" to him that the Fanjuls are not U.S. citizens. "If someone comes to the county asking to be considered for minority status, we accept their representations that they are exactly that."[12]

Of course, most immigrants are not like the Fanjuls, whose fortune exceeds $500 million. Most immigrants come here simply because America is — well, America. But immigration since the late 1960s has swollen the ranks of Hispanics and Asians, making them, combined, more numerous than blacks. As a result, we now face the prospect (especially in our largest cities, where the Hispanic and Asian populations are most concentrated) of increasing conflict among affirmative action groups.

Los Angeles, a city being dramatically reshaped by Hispanic immigration, is a case in point. In 1988 the Los Angeles County Office of Affirmative Action Compliance issued a report showing that while Hispanics made up 27.6 percent of the county population and held 18.3 percent of county jobs, blacks constituted 12.6 percent of the population and 30 percent of the workforce. The county board of supervisors accepted the affirmative action office's recommendation to hire minorities in accordance with a scheme of "population parity."[13] This meant members of the "underrepresented" group — that is, Hispanics — would be preferred over those belonging to the "overrepresented" group — blacks. Black county employees quickly protested, declaring their opposition to preferential treatment based on race and ethnicity. Over the years the struggle has continued, and now the county is thinking about dropping population parity in favor of an affirmative action approach that would result in fewer preferences for Hispanics, whose portion of the county population has risen to 38 percent. To prevent this change, Hispanic county employees have filed a lawsuit.[14]

The impact of immigration is another reason to reevaluate

affirmative action. We can choose to stick with the status quo, perhaps mending it a bit here and there, or we can end affirmative action once and for all. The choice was clarified politically in the months following the 1994 midterm elections in which the Republicans, for the first time in forty years, captured both houses of Congress. Though the campaign was not explicitly about affirmative action, the election results necessarily altered the nation's political agenda, pushing it in a more conservative direction. In California, organizers of a 1996 ballot initiative that would ban preferences on the part of state and local governments intensified their efforts. In Washington, the new Congress voted to terminate a seventeen-year-old program under which corporations selling their broadcast outlets at a discounted price to minorities may defer sales taxes indefinitely. President Clinton, sensing the shift in political sentiment, signed the bill into law. Senator Robert Dole, preparing to draft legislation on affirmative action, asked the Congressional Research Service (CRS) to supply him with a list of programs containing preferences for minorities or women, whereupon President Clinton ordered his own review of government programs. Both branches of government had a lot to digest—the CRS reported to Dole more than 160 federal programs that might be construed as requiring or authorizing or encouraging preferences.

And then on June 12, 1995, the Supreme Court handed down its decision in the case involving Randy Pech. In *Adarand Constructors* v. *Pena*, the Court held that federal affirmative action programs must be held to a standard of "strict scrutiny," the most demanding level of justification, whose application routinely has led to the invalidation of governmental measures that classify on the basis of race and ethnicity.[15] Sending Randy Pech's case back to the lower courts for review under the tougher standard, the Court signaled that preferential treatment deserves not only strict judicial scrutiny but also strict political scrutiny, since the very idea that government should distinguish on the basis of race to confer or deny a benefit is at odds with our best principles as a nation. No fewer than four times did Justice Sandra Day O'Connor, who wrote the Court's opinion, refer to the luminous passage in the 1943 *Hirabayashi* decision: "Distinctions between citizens solely because of their ancestry are by their very nature odious to a free people whose institutions are founded upon the doctrine of equality." O'Connor emphasized that the Constitution protects "*persons*, not *groups*," and that "all governmental action based on race" is a "*group* classification" that should be examined to make sure that "personal" rights have been protected.

Affirmative action broke with the colorblind tradition, one acknowledged in the Japanese Relocation Cases. Indeed, this tradition stretches back to the American founding. In making the choice before us about the future of affirmative action, it is imperative that we as a nation return to the place from which we began, and understand afresh the compelling and true case for colorblind justice.

2

The Fight for Colorblind Law

Supporters of affirmative action contend that our society is not colorblind, so it is naive to think the law should be. While it is true that we are not a colorblind nation, that fact cannot settle the question of what kind of law we should have. Should the law give effect to racial views? Should it acknowledge and enforce racial distinctions? And if so, which ones?

In the 1950s and early 1960s, America's civil rights leaders argued that the law should not give effect to any racial views at all and that all persons should be judged, as Martin Luther King, Jr., famously stated, "not by the color of their skin but by the content of their character." Dr. King and his allies stood solidly for the colorblind treatment of individuals, and they were gratified whenever the law inched toward colorblindness, which it did on many occasions. The most dramatic movement in that direction came in 1964, when Congress passed the Civil Rights Act.

In the latter half of the 1960s, when the architects of affirmative action began their work, they had to loosen the constraints of colorblind law and morality, for otherwise it would not have been possible to establish public policies that treat blacks differently. Once this crucial first step had been taken, preferential affirmative action could evolve into an enterprise aimed at securing more equal outcomes for certain other minority groups and also women.

The founders of affirmative action tended to describe the departure from colorblind law as "temporary." It would have been shocking had they said that affirmative action was going to be permanent, for colorblindness lay then, as it still does today, at the core of American ideals.

Up from Slavery—and from Racial Distinctions

The idea of colorblind law has its deepest roots in the founding principles of the nation. The ringing language of the Declaration of Independence—"We hold these truths to be self-evident, that all men are created equal, that they are endowed by their Creator with certain unalienable rights, that among these are Life, Liberty, and the pursuit of Happiness"—may have been inspired by contemporary notions of the rights of Englishmen, but it applied pointedly to *all* men, as individuals. In founding the nation on the principle of the equality of all men, the Declaration thus provided slaves with a reason to flee their masters and abolitionists with a text to argue their case against slavery. For if all men are born equally in possession of the same rights, surely one of these is the right to freedom from enslavement by another man. In 1778, the

Quaker abolitionist Anthony Benezet observed that "nothing can more clearly and positively militate against the slavery of the Negroes" than the libertarian ideals of the Declaration of Independence.[1]

We know the tragic history that ensued. The Constitution compromised on slavery, forbidding Congress to prohibit the importation of slaves until 1808 and allowing the states to decide for themselves whether to abolish or retain the "peculiar institution." The demise of slavery was tragically slow in coming, and required a civil war in which 620,000 Americans died—more than in all of our other wars combined.

The founding principle of equality played a critical role in the nation's effort to rid itself of slavery. Taking issue with the Supreme Court's notorious 1857 decision in the *Dred Scott* case, which held (among other things) that slaves were property protected by the Constitution, Abraham Lincoln insisted that blacks are men, and that as men they therefore are created equal, "entitled to all the natural rights enumerated in the Declaration of Independence."[2] Lincoln argued that no man could ever legitimately exercise his natural right to self-government by enslaving another man, because natural rights belong equally to all, at birth. "As I would not be a slave, so I would not be a master," he said. "This expresses my idea of democracy. Whatever differs from this, to the extent of the difference, is not democracy."[3]

Lincoln understood that the Declaration provided a compelling argument against slavery. But he also knew that the document was silent as to how a legal system should treat citizens. Still, the Declaration did hold out the possibility that *anyone* could become an American—the nation plainly was not founded on racial or ethnic or religious lines—and some blacks had become citizens of northern states. Thus, the kind of legal system most consistent with the founding principles seemed to be one that would treat all citizens equally, whoever they may be, whatever their race or ethnic background. In retrospect, it is not surprising that in the first half of the nineteenth century abolitionists in the North, moved by principles of equality, took aim at laws in their states that subjected blacks to legal disabilities. In Ohio, for example, abolitionists worked to eliminate laws denying blacks the right to vote and barring black children from attending public schools.

It was in opposition to laws prohibiting marriage between persons of different races that the argument for colorblind law first emerged. An early nineteenth-century Massachusetts statute forbade marriage between a white person and "a negro, indian or mulatto." In 1839, the Lynn Women's Anti-Slavery Society of Lynn, Massachusetts, objected to this law because it drew distinctions on the basis of race.[4] The Lynn women made their case to the legislature, which eventually decided to repeal the law.

In the 1850 case of *Roberts* v. *Boston*, lawyer Charles Sumner argued along similar lines when he represented a four-year-old black girl named Sarah Roberts who had been denied admission to the primary school nearest her home under a Massachusetts law requiring racially segregated public schools. Sumner contended that the "fact that a child is black, or that he is white, cannot of itself be considered a qualification, or disqualification. It is not to the skin that we can look for the criterion of fitness for our public schools." Arguing that the state law conflicted with the state constitution's guarantee of "equality before the law," Sumner maintained that school authorities should not have the discretion to assign children on the basis of race to different schools because they cannot "assume, a priori, and without individual examination, that an entire race possess certain moral or intellectual qualities, which shall render it proper to place them all in a class by themselves."[5]

Sumner failed to persuade the court that the constitutional guarantee of equality meant that the state could not distinguish citizens on the basis of race and assign them to different schools. But his position soon triumphed. In 1855, the Massachusetts legislature ended public school segregation by enacting a colorblind statute, which provided: "In determining the qualifications of scholars to be admitted into any public school or any district school in the Commonwealth, no distinction shall be made on account of the race, color, or religious opinions, of the applicant or scholar." The new law provided for damages for anyone excluded from a school on the basis of one of these now forbidden grounds.

The abolitionists, who were motivated by the cruelty of slavery as well as by the degrading treatment of blacks outside the South, had more than one argument for opposing laws distinguishing on the basis of race. Some abolitionists, drawing on their faith, contended that man's laws should make no distinctions not found in God's law—and God's law did not distinguish on the basis of race and in fact commanded impartial treatment of all persons. But the argument that would echo down through the years was the specifically legal one made by Sumner and others—that laws drawing distinctions based upon race could never produce equal treatment and secure equal rights. This argument did not maintain that racial distinctions were necessarily unfounded, only that such distinctions would lead to morally objectionable differences in treatment—discrimination, in modern terms. The upshot of the argument was that government should not have the power to classify or sort citizens on the basis of race.[6] Government should be, in short, colorblind.

The issues that the abolitionists grappled with in Ohio and Massachusetts before the Civil War were on the nation's agenda soon thereafter. With slavery forever outlawed by the Thirteenth Amendment, ratified in December 1865, Congress moved to secure rights of the four million former slaves. The Civil Rights Act of 1866, passed over President Andrew Johnson's veto, accorded all persons the same civil rights, which included the rights of personal security and personal liberty, and the right to acquire and enjoy property. Specifically, the law gave citizens "of every race and color" the same right to make contracts; sue; testify in court; purchase, hold, and dispose of property; and to enjoy "full and equal benefit of all laws." Because of doubts about the law's constitutionality, Congress incorporated its protections into the Fourteenth Amendment, which, ratified in 1868, explicitly guarantees "the equal protection of the laws." Two years later came the Fifteenth Amendment, which protects the right to vote against racial discrimination.

During this period in which we improved our Constitution, the former abolitionists pressed for an amendment that in no uncertain terms would have made the Constitution colorblind. Wendell Phillips, a prominent Boston abolitionist, led the effort. His proposed amendment reflected the abiding concern of abolitionists over the previous quarter century—namely, that government should not even distinguish on the basis of race. "No State," the amendment read, "shall make any distinction among its citizens on account of race and color."[7] The point of Phillips's amendment was in the plainest terms possible to deny to state governments the ability to engage in racial regulation of any kind, no matter how reasonable it might seem to whoever might be in power. Phillips said that his amendment would establish nothing less than "a government color-blind."

By the 1880s, laws distinguishing on the basis of color and discriminating against blacks had begun to spread throughout the South. Hopes for colorblind law were dashed in 1896, when the Supreme Court sanctioned state-imposed "Jim Crow" segregation in *Plessy* v. *Ferguson*.[8] The law at issue in the case had been enacted by the Louisiana legislature in 1890 and required "equal but separate accommodations" aboard passenger trains "for the white and colored races." A person who insisted on occupying a coach or compartment "other than the one set apart for his race" could be fined or even imprisoned. Integration by the free choices of individuals was not just illegal but criminal. Homer Plessy, the man who challenged the law, had purchased a first-class ticket on the East Louisiana Railway, en route from New Orleans to Covington. Though Plessy was one-eighth black, he took a seat in the car reserved for whites, refusing the conductor's order that he move to the car reserved for "colored" persons. Plessy was forcibly ejected from the train and placed in the hands of New Orleans law enforcement authorities. In his lawsuit, Plessy claimed that the railcar law had violated his Fourteenth Amendment right to "the equal protection of the laws." However, the Louisiana Supreme Court said that the law was constitutional, and the U.S. Supreme Court agreed. Justice Henry Billings Brown, writing for a majority of seven justices, said that the legally imposed segregation of the races on passenger trains did not violate the equal protection clause of the Fourteenth Amendment. So long as the separate facilities were "equal," the Louisiana statute amounted to what he called a "reasonable regulation."

In his dissent, Justice John Paul Harlan declared: "In respect of civil rights, common to all citizens, the Constitution of the United States does not, I think, permit the public authority to know the race of those entitled to be protected in the enjoyment of such rights." Summarizing his point, he said, "Our constitution is color-blind, and neither knows nor tolerates classes among citizens."

For Harlan, the equal protection of the laws meant that government may not classify on the basis of race, regardless of how "reasonable" any classification might seem. His interpretation was not grounded in an explication of the text or history of the Constitution but in a practical assessment of the nation's needs. "The destinies of the two races, in this country, are indissolubly linked together," he wrote, "and the interests of both require that the common government of all shall not permit the seeds of race hate to be planted under the sanction of law."[9]

In arguing that government should not have the authority to engage in racial regulation of any kind, Harlan made clear that by "government" he also meant the judiciary. "I deny," he wrote, "that any legislative body or judicial tribunal may have regard to the race of citizens when the civil rights of those citizens are involved." For Harlan, not only should the elective branches not pass laws distinguishing on the basis of race, but the courts should not be in the position of having to decide whether such laws were "reasonable" enough to be deemed constitutional. The whole business, he argued, should be off-limits to government.

Harlan's opinion, however, did not carry the day; he could not persuade even one of his fellow justices to endorse his position. But if the majority opinion in *Plessy* represented a low point in the fight for colorblind law, Harlan's dissent was not wasted ink. His opinion would later inspire the leaders of the civil rights movement as they battled successfully against segregation and other forms of racial discrimination.

No Distinction . . . No Discrimination

At the outset of World War II, A. Philip Randolph, president of the Brotherhood of Sleeping Car Porters, led a march on Washington seeking an end to employment discrimination against blacks. American soldiers, many of whom were black, were waging war against fascism abroad and yet blacks in the United States were subject to unequal treatment—facts duly noted in the international press. Taking aim at a prominent segregationist governor, Randolph shrewdly asked, "What's the difference between Hitler and that 'cracker' Talmadge from Georgia?" Randolph invoked the colorblind tradition, as he sought "the abrogation of every law which makes a distinction in treatment between citizens based on religion, creed, color, or national origin."[10]

President Franklin D. Roosevelt responded to Randolph's march by issuing Executive Order 8802, which set forth "the policy of the United States that there shall be no discrimination in the employment of workers in defense industries or government because of race, creed, color, or national origin." The executive order required all government departments and agencies with vocational and training programs for defense production to make sure that the programs were administered "without discrimination because of race, creed, or national origin." It mandated the inclusion in all defense contracts of "a provision obligating the contractor not to discriminate against any worker because of race, creed, color, or national origin." And it created a Committee on Fair Employment Practice with the authority to investigate complaints of discrimination and recommend appropriate remedies.

By acting on the basis of an executive order, Roosevelt set a precedent for presidential involvement in securing civil rights. His successor stayed the new course. In February 1948, President Harry Truman asked Congress to enact legislation "prohibiting discrimination in employment based on race, color, religion, or national origin." Congress failed to do so, but Truman had started the process that would culminate in the passage of the Civil Rights Act of 1964. Also in 1948, Truman, relying on his constitutional authority as commander-in-chief, issued an executive order ending racial discrimination in the armed services. The executive order declared "the policy of the President that there shall be equality of treatment and opportunity for all persons in the armed forces without regard to race, color, religion, or national origin."

The Supreme Court, meanwhile, was being asked whether racial discrimination by government violates the Constitution. Military curfew and exclusion orders issued in the wake of Pearl Harbor resulted in the wartime internment of American citizens of Japanese ancestry. In *Hirabayashi* v. *United States* (1943) and *Korematsu* v. *United States* (1944), the Supreme Court declined to strike down the orders, agreeing with the executive branch that the exigencies of war permitted such exceptional measures.[11] But the Japanese Relocation Cases at the same time drew from the Court a vigorous statement of colorblind principle, arguably its most splendid ever. Despite failing to vindicate the rights of the Japanese Americans, the majority in the *Hirabayashi* case declared, "Distinctions between citizens solely because of their ancestry are by their very nature odious to a free people whose institutions are founded upon the doctrine of equality," adding that "in other and most circumstances racial distinctions are irrelevant." In his dissent in the *Korematsu* case, Justice Frank Murphy went a step further in saying that there was *no* circumstance, not even wartime, in which distinctions drawn on the basis of race could be accepted. "Racial discrimination in any form and in any degree," he wrote, "has no justifiable part whatever in our democratic way of life."

Imagine how the lawyers for the NAACP Legal Defense Fund must have reacted upon reading these statements of colorblind law. Starting in the 1930s, those lawyers had embarked upon a litigation strategy designed to end public school segregation. The NAACP strategy was to show that separate schools for blacks could never be equal, but emboldened by the colorblind sentiments expressed by Justices Stone and Murphy in the Japanese Relocation Cases, the organization's lawyers decided to advance a full-throated argument for a colorblind Constitution. Notably, they were not deterred by the fact that the institutions and the governments and indeed the society they challenged were obviously not colorblind. The NAACP lawyers pressed the colorblind argument in a series of cases in which the Court ruled in behalf of their clients.

The first attempt came in the 1948 case of *Sipuel* v. *Board of Regents of the University of Oklahoma.*[12] Successfully challenging the decision by the university's law school to deny admission to a black applicant while the state created a separate law school for black students, the NAACP's Thurgood Marshall argued that "classifications and distinctions based on race or color have no moral or legal validity in our society." Two years later, in another victory in a "separate-but-equal" case involving higher education, Marshall and his colleagues told the Court in *McLaurin* v. *Oklahoma State Regents for Higher Education* that "racial classification by government is unconstitutional."[13] The *McLaurin* case was decided together with a case involving the constitutionality of the state of Texas's creation of a makeshift law school for blacks, *Sweatt* v. *Painter.*[14] The NAACP Legal Defense Fund divided its argument with the Committee of Law Teachers Against

Segregation in Legal Education. In a friend-of-the-court brief, which drew proudly upon Harlan's dissent in *Plessy* v. *Ferguson,* the organization elaborated an argument for color-blind constitutional law that made the by now familiar connection between racial distinctions and racial discrimination:

> Laws which give equal protection are those which make no discrimination because of race in the sense that they make no distinction because of race. As soon as laws make a right or responsibility dependent solely on race, they violate the Fourteenth Amendment. Reasonable classifications may be made, but one basis of classification is completely precluded; for the Equal Protection Clause makes racial classifications unreasonable per se.[15]

Colorblind law also won the support of the government's chief litigator—the solicitor general. In a 1950 case involving the constitutionality of segregated dining cars operated with the federal government's approval, he argued: "Racial discriminations effected by action of the Federal Government, or any agency thereof, are prohibited by the due process clause of the Fifth Amendment."[16]

In each of these four cases the Supreme Court ruled against segregation, whittling away its legal justification. Though the Court did not rest its decisions on the colorblind argument, this fact did not discourage Thurgood Marshall and his colleagues. And in 1954, in *Brown* v. *Board of Education,* they made their most vigorous effort yet in behalf of colorblind constitutional law.[17]

The four cases consolidated in *Brown* raised the "separate-but-equal" question in the context of primary and secondary education. The issue was whether the Constitution allows racially segregated public schools. The NAACP's lawyers told the Court: "It is [our] thesis . . . [that] the Fourteenth Amend-

ment prevents states from according differential treatment to
American children on the basis of their color or race. . . . Distinctions drawn by state authorities on the basis of color or
race violate the Fourteenth Amendment. . . . The broad general purpose of the Amendment [is the] obliteration of race
and color distinctions."[18] The lawyers added, "that the Constitution is colorblind is our dedicated belief."

On May 17, 1954, the Court issued its unanimous ruling in
Brown, declaring that "in the field of public education the
doctrine of 'separate-but-equal' has no place. Separate educational facilities are inherently unequal" and consequently
in violation of the Constitution. The Court again did not base
its conclusion on the colorblind argument it was offered.
Had it done so, affirmative action could not have begun without *Brown*'s qualification, for government-sponsored affirmative action programs that purport to make "reasonable
classifications" based on race would not have been possible
under a colorblind Constitution. At the time of *Brown,* of
course, no one could have anticipated future events. And
because the result in *Brown* was consistent with colorblind
norms then being preached by the political leaders of the
civil rights movement, the decision was widely interpreted in
those terms. The *New York Times* even told its readers that
"the words [Justice Harlan] used in his lonely dissent [in
Plessy] . . . have become in effect . . . a part of the law of the
land." Over the next few years, the Court continued to erase
the color line, as it invalidated segregation in public parks,
beaches and recreational facilities, and in public transportation, each time citing *Brown* in memorandum opinions.

The Court's midcentury decisions against discrimination
were bold advances on the measures Presidents Roosevelt
and Truman had taken to secure the same result in defense
contracting and in the military. Numerous states, meanwhile,

had passed fair employment laws also aimed at ensuring nondiscrimination. Leading politicians also began speaking out for the colorblind treatment of individuals. At the NAACP Convention in 1952, for example, Senator Hubert Humphrey of Minnesota declared, "There is no room for any aristocracy in America. Our democratic principle is one of judging men on their merit, not by their race."

The old idea that persons could be judged on the basis of skin color was plainly in retreat. And thanks to radio and television, Americans everywhere became acquainted with the demonstrated excellence of black Americans in numerous fields of endeavor. Charles Drew's pioneering work in hematology led to the establishment of the American Red Cross. Ralph Bunche, the undersecretary of the United Nations, mediated the 1948–49 Arab-Israeli War and was awarded the 1950 Nobel Peace Prize. Then, too, there was the legion of black Americans who lit up the stage and the screen, and who dominated sports. No one could listen to Marian Anderson sing or Sammy Davis, Jr., perform and fail to see the excellence of their performances. Nor was it possible to watch the total baseball package that was Jackie Robinson and not realize that here was a player destined for the Hall of Fame.

During the 1950s, the modern civil rights movement led by Martin Luther King, Jr., undertook as a complement to its legal strategies a social protest effort grounded in religious faith that was designed to defeat segregation and advance the principle of nondiscrimination. The boycotts, sit-ins, and other demonstrations that commenced with Rosa Parks's refusal in 1955 to yield her bus seat to a white rider focused relentlessly on the immorality of racial discrimination. The movement emphatically condemned the tendency to classify and judge people in terms of race.

The civil rights movement captured the moral high ground in American politics. People of every skin color or race could see the truth of the position advanced with honor and dignity throughout the South. As Shelby Steele has pointed out in *The Content of Our Character,* "in Montgomery, Little Rock, and Selma, racial power was the enemy and moral power the weapon." And because Jim Crow was morally indefensible, the tortuous rationalizations for treating people differently according to race, which for so long supported the subjugation and degradation of blacks, ultimately were seen for what they were. In calling upon whites "to be moral" (Steele's plain-spoken phrase), the civil rights movement wielded the most potent weapon there was against racial discrimination.[19]

The Triumph of Colorblind Law

In early 1961, President Kennedy, who had endorsed the student sit-ins initiated the year before and pledged his commitment to the moral cause of civil rights, issued Executive Order 10925, which prohibited discrimination on account of "race, creed, color, or national origin" in federal employment and on the part of private employers doing business with the government. Two years later, on February 28, 1963, Kennedy delivered a special message to Congress that began by invoking Justice Harlan—"Our constitution is color-blind, and neither knows nor tolerates classes among citizens." These words governed the recommendation Kennedy eventually made to Congress that year, which became the Civil Rights Act of 1964. On June 11, 1963, in a nationally televised speech, Kennedy expanded on his February 28 address, appealing to the founding principle "that all men are created equal" and contending that "the rights of everyone are diminished when the rights of one man are threatened." In a restatement of the color-blind principle, Kennedy told viewers that it should be possible "for every American to enjoy the privileges of being an American without regard to his race or his color. In short, every American ought to have the right to be treated as he would wish to be treated, as one would wish his children to be treated." Kennedy stated his intention to ask Congress "to make a commitment" to the proposition "that race has no place in American life or law."

On June 19, Kennedy sent to Congress legislation requiring nondiscrimination in public accommodations, public education, federally assisted programs, and voting rights. (Provisions covering private employment were added the next year.) As the legislation began to move through Congress, civil rights leaders chose August 28 to hold a march in Washington. The event provided the occasion for one of the great orations in American history, Martin Luther King's "I Have a Dream" speech. Declaring that his dream is "deeply rooted in the American dream," King preached these words: "I have a dream that one day this nation will rise up and live out the true meaning of its creed: 'We hold these truths to be self-evident, that all men are created equal.'" King went on to declare what it would mean to live out "the true meaning" of our founding creed when he said that in his dream "my four little children" will live "in a nation where they will not be judged by the color of their skin but by the content of their character." Afterwards, when civil rights leaders met with President Kennedy, he, too, spoke from the colorblind tradition, reiterating his intention to secure "equal treatment and equal opportunity for all without regard to race, color, creed, or nationality."

Signed into law by President Lyndon Johnson, the Civil Rights Act of 1964 comprehensively legislated the principle of nondiscrimination by outlawing racial discrimination in public accommodations, public education, federally assisted programs, and most private employment. Indeed, the "sonorous phrases" of the nondiscrimination principle, Harvard University's Nathan Glazer observes, sound richly throughout the legislation: no discrimination "on the ground of race, color, religion or national origin" (Titles II and VI, concerning public accommodations and federally funded programs, respectively); no discrimination "on account of . . . race, color, religion, or national origin" (Title III, concerning public facilities); no discrimination "by reason of race, color, religion, or national origin" (Title IV, concerning public education); and no discrimination "because of . . . color, religion, sex, or national origin" (Title VII, concerning private employment).[20]

The new law embodied the same definition of discrimination that earlier advocates of colorblind law had advanced. As Senator Clifford P. Case of New Jersey put it during the congressional debate over Title VII, discrimination means "a distinction [or] . . . difference in treatment or favor" based on "the forbidden" criterion of race.[21] And by plainly rejecting the notion that people may be treated in terms of race, the law invited Americans to regard each other as individuals, without regard to race. Clearly, the Civil Rights Act of 1964, together with the Voting Rights Act of 1965, which ensured nondiscriminatory access to the ballot, marked the greatest triumph to date of the generations of Americans who had fought for colorblind law and morality.

Summarizing that effort, Andrew Kull of the Emory Law School writes that "over a period of some 125 years . . . the American civil rights movement first elaborated, then held as its unvarying political objective, a rule of law requiring the color-blind treatment of individuals." During this period, Kull says, "the right of the individual to be treated without regard to race was strenuously defended as a moral and political end in itself."[22] It was defended by Americans drawing on the principles of the Enlightenment as well as the Jewish and Christian traditions stretching back over more than two millennia. William Van Alstyne of the Duke University Law School has captured well the moral reason that individuals should be treated without regard to race: "Individuals are not merely social means; i.e., they are not merely examples of a group, representatives of a cohort, or fungible surrogates of other human beings; each, rather, is a person whom it is improper to count or discount by race."[23]

Soon after the Civil Rights Act of 1964 became law, however, the idea began to gain currency, especially in government and academe, that colorblind law and morality was too constraining, that the public and private sector alike needed to be able to make racial distinctions—benign ones, to be sure. A profound shift in elite opinion was taking place. Affirmative action was about to be born.

3

Shackled Runners:
The Rise of Affirmative Action

On June 4, 1965, President
Lyndon Johnson delivered the commencement speech at
Howard University. Congress was about to pass the Voting
Rights Act, and the President duly celebrated the new law.
But his remarks to the audience of about 5,000 were mainly
about the future of black Americans:

> Freedom is not enough. You do not wipe away the scars of
> centuries by saying now you're free to go where you want
> and do as you desire and choose the leaders you please.
> You do not take a person who for years has been hobbled
> by chains and liberate him, bring him up to the starting
> line of a race and then say, you're free to compete with all

the others, and justly believe that you have been completely
fair. . . . It is not enough just to open the gates of opportunity. All our citizens must have the ability to walk through
those gates.

In what Johnson called "the next and the more profound
stage of civil rights," the object would be "not just freedom
but opportunity—not just legal equity but human ability—
not just equality as a right and a theory but equality as a fact
and equality as a result."

Johnson cited statistics showing blacks lagging behind
whites on a number of measures, such as employment. He
dwelt on "the breakdown of the Negro family structure." But
the socioeconomic condition of blacks wasn't their fault, he
emphasized, noting the centuries of slavery and segregation.
The President placed on whites the moral duty to remedy the
nation's "one huge wrong," and he said that the federal government would take the lead. Black poverty was being attacked
through "our poverty programs, our education programs, our
health program and a dozen more." They would be expanded,
he declared, "until this most enduring of foes yields to our
unyielding will." Johnson promised other government programs to strengthen black families, and called for a conference later in the summer that would continue the work of
this "more profound stage of civil rights." Through these
means, Johnson said, the nation would pursue "equality as a
result" and do justice for a racial group so long denied it.

Over the next decade and more, the federal government
pursued parts of this agenda. The social welfare expenditures
Johnson prescribed began during his tenure and shot up
dramatically during the 1970s. But the pursuit of justice also
required something Johnson did not mention in his
speech—the abandonment of colorblind law and principle.

The big issue in those days—it had been since the *Brown* decision—was school desegregation, and in 1966 the Johnson administration issued guidelines that all but endorsed the idea of making pupil assignments on the basis of race. Influential opinions written by Judge John Minor Wisdom for the Fifth Circuit Court of Appeals gave the guidelines a broad interpretation. Wisdom, who in 1959 and than again in 1964 had written opinions explicitly endorsing a colorblind Constitution, wrote that remedying segregation requires a color-conscious Constitution because only that can prevent the perpetuation of discrimination and undo its present effects.[1] Beginning in the late 1960s, the NAACP Legal Defense Fund, having argued in the Supreme Court as recently as 1963 that the Constitution is colorblind, routinely endorsed involuntary, race-based busing as a remedy for desegregation.[2] And, in the 1971 case of *Swann* v. *Charlotte-Mecklenburg Board of Education,* the Court unanimously upheld a lower court order imposing busing on the public school system in Charlotte, North Carolina.[3]

Other policies also led to the suspension of colorblind law. But the most controversial and the one affecting by far the largest number of Americans was affirmative action.

Johnson didn't mention affirmative action in his speech, but the metaphor of the shackled runner unable to compete inspired the designers of the new policy. To overcome the legacy of slavery and segregation, went the original argument for affirmative action, we must temporarily treat blacks not equally but differently, by taking their race into account in allocating opportunity. No one knew how long this temporary period would be, but the premises of the policy suggested that affirmative action could not end until the achievement of "equality as a result"—an equality statistically demonstrated, as when roughly the same percentage of blacks as whites were going to the best schools and getting the best jobs. As Jesse Jackson would later put it, "Equality can be measured. It can be put into numbers."[4]

Lyndon Johnson was one of the founding fathers of affirmative action, and so was his successor, Richard Nixon. The creation, development, and consolidation of affirmative action was a bipartisan affair with Republicans no less than Democrats contributing to its establishment. The new policy advanced not just in the federal government but also in the states, and not just in the public sector but in the private sector, too. Along the way it encompassed other racial and ethnic groups, and also women, and it acquired justifications other than the original remedial one. By the end of the 1970s, the policy cleared its last hurdle when the Supreme Court refused to condemn affirmative action for its departure from colorblind principles.

The Turn

In his front-page story on Johnson's Howard speech, *New York Times* reporter Tom Wicker noted that the President had not explicitly mentioned what civil rights leaders now desired—quotas and preferences. Obviously, a turn in their thinking had occurred that was sharp and sudden. It is hard to find in the speeches or statements of civil rights leaders prior to the early 1960s any sustained interest in "preferential treatment" for blacks. In 1961, the northern chapters of the Congress of Racial Equality (CORE) decided that nondiscrimination was not enough and told the banks, contractors, and manufacturers they picketed and boycotted to adopt racial preferences in their hiring practices. This became CORE's national policy by the end of 1962. But CORE represented a small minority within the civil rights community.

In a congressional hearing in 1963, even CORE's own James Farmer declined to defend publicly his organization's shift to preferences.[5]

Whitney Young, head of the National Urban League, also was an early supporter of preferences. He believed that "a decade of discrimination in favor of Negro youth" was needed to make up for "300 years of deprivation." But when he tried to persuade the league's board of trustees to endorse "a compensatory, preferential Marshall Plan for black America," he met with overwhelming, principled opposition. The president of the Urban League in Pittsburgh framed the kind of question he thought the public would ask: "What in blazes are these guys up to? They tell us for years that we must buy [nondiscrimination] and then say, 'It isn't what we want.'" A member of the Urban League in New York objected to what he called "the heart of it"—"the business of employing Negroes 'because they are Negroes.'"[6] Young wound up calling for an antipoverty coalition formed along nonracial lines. The prevailing view among liberals and civil rights leaders at that time was still strongly in favor of colorblind law.

Looking back, we can see how they changed their minds. Black leaders historically had sought equal laws as well as an improvement in the condition of blacks generally. The civil rights movement dating from the 1930s had been preoccupied with the first goal, and once it was achieved (through court decisions and statutes including the Civil Rights Act of 1964 and the Voting Rights Act of 1965), social and economic improvement absorbed their attention. Martin Luther King, Jr., anticipated this shift in his speech on the Washington Mall on August 28, 1963. The speech climaxed a march in behalf of "Jobs and Freedom." Note that "jobs" came first, even though the event itself had the near-term objective of securing the Civil Rights Act. And in King's speech, remembered for its soaring admonition that we should treat one another without regard to race, he also observed that "the Negro lives on a lonely island of poverty in the midst of a vast ocean of material prosperity."

By the time Johnson gave his Howard commencement address, the goal of ameliorating the condition of blacks had begun to draw the attention of the influential—not only the President and his subordinates in government but also federal judges and leaders in education, the media, publishing, the foundation world—the elites of the time. Old assumptions about public policy yielded to entirely new ones: poverty now was a substantial concern of the federal government where before it had not been. Where colorblindness had been a worthy moral and legal goal, it was now deemed necessary to put it aside, at least temporarily, if the nation were to achieve justice for blacks, the poorest group among us. And this justice must be measured ultimately in terms of results—of how blacks as a group were doing compared with the majority white society. According to the new paradigm for civil rights policy, colorblind equal opportunity could not by itself produce equal results. Not only did blacks need special help to overcome the effects of past discrimination, but the American social and economic system was inherently discriminatory.[7] The system would therefore perpetuate the sins of the past unless it were changed, and it could be changed only if the public and private sector alike began "taking race into account."

The interpretation placed on the inner-city race riots of the 1960s confirmed the turn in elite opinion. The traditional response to a riot had been to hold the rioting individuals responsible for their actions, but that did not happen in this case, as the riots were seen as a necessary and even just response to what whites had done to blacks historically. In

1968, the National Advisory Commission on Civil Disorders appointed by President Johnson, familiarly known as the Kerner Commission, explicitly held "white racism" responsible "for the explosive mixture which has been accumulating in our cities since the end of World War II."[8] The riots were understood to ask the question: What were we as a nation going to do, now, to make amends?

A large part of the answer was affirmative action. By no means did all of those seeking to better the condition of blacks agree with it. For example, Bayard Rustin, the deputy director of the 1963 "Jobs and Freedom" march, voiced his opposition to preferences in a February 1965 article in *Commentary*. But within the civil rights establishment and among political liberals generally, Rustin's views were held by a shrinking minority. The idea of using race to get beyond racism had taken hold.

The Johnson Era: First Steps

The Johnson administration pursued affirmative action in the private economy. It did so first through law enforcement that is better described as law transformation, and second, through the creation of new law.

Title VII of the Civil Rights Act of 1964 forbids discrimination in employment on account of "race, color, religion, sex, or national origin." According to its text and history, Title VII outlawed *intentional* discrimination against *individuals*. But the Equal Employment Opportunity Commission (EEOC), the bureaucracy charged with enforcing Title VII, concluded soon after it opened for business in the summer of 1965 that if the statute were enforced according to its original terms, it would do little to increase black employment and improve race relations. Proving discrimination in terms of bad motive would often be hard, officials believed, because intent can be difficult to pin down. And if this were all Title VII were good for, as one of the agency's first officials, Alfred Blumrosen, later wrote, "the plight of racial and ethnic minorities must be attributable to some more generalized failures in society, in the fields of basic education, housing, family relations, and the like." Dealing effectively with the problems in these "general and difficult areas," he implied, would simply take too long. If, however, Title VII could be used to attack discrimination "broadly defined" as encompassing "all conduct which adversely affects minority group employment opportunities," said Blumrosen, "then the prospects for rapid improvement in minority employment opportunities are greatly increased."[9] In the scenario Blumrosen envisioned, an employer who was told that his employment practices adversely affected a particular racial group—a point made through evidence of statistical disparities—could be forced to hire minorities in sufficient numbers to avoid liability.

The EEOC's effort to transform Title VII into a statute that could be used to attack discrimination "broadly defined" encountered numerous problems created by the original meaning of Title VII, yet none proved insuperable. To infer discrimination from unequal group outcomes, the EEOC needed employment data showing the distribution of minorities and women in a given employer's workforce. Title VII, however, exempted from the usual record-keeping and reporting requirements all employers already reporting information about their workforces to state and local antidiscrimination agencies and also to the U.S. Labor Department. But the creative Blumrosen proposed a uniform system of racial record-keeping and reporting that would yield the necessary data. The commission adopted his proposal, which

Blumrosen himself admitted was "contrary to the plain meaning of Title VII."[10]

The new reporting system revealed the nature of the jobs in the private sector held by minorities and women, and the data showed, among other things, that minorities held few white-collar jobs. The problem now was how to use the data to prove discrimination when there was no evidence—as Title VII required—of bad motive. Because Title VII explicitly prohibited any requirement of "preferential treatment to any individual or to any group" on account of "an imbalance which may exist" in their numbers or percentages relative to nonminorities, it did not appear that the commission could get very far using statistical evidence to force an employer to explain that he is *not* discriminating. Still, the commission thought it might be able to put employers on the defensive by claiming that statistical disparities resulted from particular employment practices, such as hiring on the basis of performance on a paper-and-pencil test. This move, too, had an uncertain prospect, for Title VII explicitly protected the use of professionally developed tests and seniority systems so long as such use was not racially motivated.

Nonetheless, by 1968 the EEOC's view of Title VII enjoyed wide acceptance in the civil rights community and had the support of plaintiffs' lawyers. The emerging legal doctrine not only assumed that socioeconomic advancement could be realized through a lawsuit based on unequal group outcomes—"disparate impact," as it was called—but also placed on employers the responsibility for those outcomes, whatever their cause, and regardless of the employers' own motives. In sum, the disparate impact approach made employers responsible for all that had happened to the shackled runners before they got to the starting line—even before they were born.

The Johnson Labor Department also pursued affirmative action in private employment. Here, though, the law's course did not begin with a congressional statute, but with an executive order—one that explicitly requires affirmative action. In contrast, Title VII was not an affirmative action statute; it mentioned the term, without defining it, only in the provision dealing with judicial remedies for proven discrimination.

As we saw in chapter 2, starting with Franklin D. Roosevelt, presidents issued orders requiring nondiscrimination on the part of private firms that contract with the government. Johnson inherited the most recent, Executive Order 10925, issued by John F. Kennedy in 1961, which required contractors to refrain from discrimination *and* to undertake affirmative action. Officials enforcing the Kennedy order had required contractors to furnish profiles of their workforces broken down in terms of race. Also, they had asked whether blacks were sufficiently represented in a given contractor's workforce. But it was left to the Johnson administration to develop the numerical approach to affirmative action that persists still today.

In 1965, Johnson issued Executive Order 11246, which mirrored the Kennedy order almost word for word. The Johnson order located its enforcement in the Labor Department, specifically in a new subagency—the Office of Federal Contract Compliance (OFCC). The agency possessed the power of the federal contract purse, for it could withhold money if the contractor failed to do the government's bidding. Initial steps on the path to numerical affirmative action were taken in 1966 when the agency's first director, Edward Sylvester, announced that contractors wishing to bid on $125 million in hospital and school construction projects in the Cleveland area must devise affirmative action plans that "have the result of assuring that there was minority group representation in all trades on the job in all phases of the work." Sylvester thus expressed the idea of proportional representation that would shape subsequent enforcement of the executive order. In response to his announcement, one contractor seeking the work offered to provide a "manning table" that would indicate the specific number of minority workers to be hired in each trade. As historian Hugh Davis Graham explains in *The Civil Rights Era*, the table "amounted to a contractor's promissory note that if he was awarded the job, he would hire X number of minority workers." The OFCC awarded the contract and promptly decided to urge manning tables on all other firms bidding for contracts in the Cleveland area.[11]

Later that year the OFCC sought to integrate the construction trades unions in Philadelphia by demanding manning tables that embodied the same proportionalist idea from contractors bidding on federal contracts. Willard Wirtz, Johnson's secretary of labor, denied that the numerical requirements in Cleveland or Philadelphia would become general policy. The two situations, he said, were exceptional because there was "probably no effective alternative" to the use of manning tables.[12] But the tables drew vigorous objections from builders and unions as well as some members of Congress. In 1968, opponents of the implicit racial preferences of the manning tables found an ally in Comptroller General Elmer Staats, who ruled that the enforcement actions in Cleveland and Philadelphia violated requirements for competitive bidding. In late November—only a few weeks after Richard Nixon's election—the Department rescinded the "Philadelphia Plan." It appeared that the Labor Department's affirmative action effort would fall by the way.

The final year of the Johnson administration also witnessed the creation of the first "set-aside" policy. In 1953,

Congress had deemed small businesses worthy of federal help when it created the Small Business Administration (SBA), an independent agency. The SBA functioned as the prime contractor for the federal government, entering into procurement contracts with the departments and agencies and then subcontracting for supplies and materials with small businesses. The SBA did not distinguish among small businesses on the ground of race or ethnicity until 1968, when it decided to interpret its statutory authority to set aside contracts for small businesses owned by "socially or economically disadvantaged" individuals. As with all of the first affirmative action steps, the SBA had fashioned its set-aside policy with blacks in mind. Specifically, the agency had acted in response to one of the conclusions of the Kerner Commission Report—namely, that "special encouragement" was needed to guide blacks into the economic mainstream.

The Nixon Era: Big Advances

In early 1968, Johnson decided not to stand for reelection. That fall Richard Nixon defeated the Democratic candidate, Vice President Hubert Humphrey. Nonetheless, affirmative action advanced dramatically.

Nixon's most significant contribution to affirmative action lay in reviving the Philadelphia Plan and then extending it. Soon after the 1968 election, Nixon designated the economist George Shultz as his secretary of labor, and Shultz, in a speech outlining his department's priorities, emphasized the need for "special measures" to employ blacks. Shultz wanted to bring back the Philadelphia Plan, and Nixon, in his memoirs, wrote that he took office wanting to do something about racial discrimination on the part of unions. It was not lost on

Nixon that the Philadelphia Plan might create tension
between two blocs of traditionally Democratic voters—union
members and blacks—that could ultimately work to his benefit in seeking a second term of office.

In reviving the Philadelphia Plan, Nixon's labor officials
had a dilemma to overcome. On the one hand, they faced the
comptroller general's objection, which was that the Labor
Department could not award a contract and then, after the
fact, press on a contractor a new requirement of specific
goals and timetables for hiring minorities. On the other
hand, they were wary of insisting on actual numbers of
minorities to be hired as part of the precontract negotiation
because Title VII of the Civil Rights Act explicitly outlawed
preferences in order to achieve racial balance. The authors of
the new plan came up with this answer: the OFCC would
establish not a specific number of minorities whom a contractor would have to hire in each area of employment but a
target "range" of minorities to be hired, expressed as a percentage that the contractor would try to meet. In the invitation for bids, the OFCC would make known what these
ranges were, and in their bids the contractors would indicate
how they might reach these targets. Because there would be
no negotiations after the bids were opened, the comptroller
general's objection would be satisfied. And because percentages would be used to define the ranges, even though they
could be translated in a moment into numbers, Title VII's
antiquota ban could not be invoked to scuttle the plan—or so
its authors believed. Anticipating future defenses of affirmative action, they maintained that the percentage goals were
not quotas, that contractors had only to make "a good faith
effort" to meet them, and that in striving to meet the goals
contractors did not have to, and indeed should not, discriminate against any qualified person.

In an effort to trump any legal argument against the new plan, Labor Solicitor Laurence H. Silberman supplied a 44-page opinion locating the legal authority for enforcement of Executive Order 11246 in the president's constitutional powers. Because the president has constitutional authority to remedy past discrimination, Silberman wrote, the Philadelphia Plan is not subject to Title VII. But, he added, even if the plan were subject to Title VII, it would still be permissible, because that statute did not explicitly prohibit the plan's racial targets.

Silberman was stretching and straining to find a way around the colorblind law of Title VII. Comptroller General Staats was not persuaded. He responded by saying that the Philadelphia Plan violated Title VII "by making race or national origin a determinative factor in employment."[13] With Nixon's backing, Labor Secretary Shultz held a press conference attacking the comptroller's view, contending that it would "destroy all reason for the existence of the executive order and the OFCC." Shultz understood that the point of having the order was indeed to make race "a determinative factor" in employment.

Attorney General John Mitchell followed with his own opinion disputing Staats. Like Silberman, Mitchell sought protection for the Philadelphia Plan in the President's constitutional powers. But Mitchell also offered a Title VII argument for the plan, contending that it was a justifiable remedy for past discrimination, similar to what judges had been ordering in Title VII cases in which discrimination had been proven. The merits of this argument to the side, the Philadelphia Plan had been unveiled in June, two months *before* the Labor Department held hearings to uncover discrimination in Philadelphia. Why, if having findings of discrimination was so important, didn't the department wait until it had them? The explanation, says historian Hugh Davis Graham, lay in the fear of riots in urban black communities.[14] The Nixon administration saw the Philadelphia Plan, which would be put into effect in most major cities, at least in part as a way to prevent another summer of violence.

The issue of whether the Philadelphia Plan was at odds with the race-blind requirements of Title VII eventually moved to the lower federal courts, which ruled that it was not.[15] With the Supreme Court declining to review the decision, the Labor Department was able to pursue affirmative action in terms of proportional representation without worrying about the pesky barks of an Elmer Staats. Yet in extending affirmative action requirements to construction contractors in other cities, and then to nonconstruction contractors everywhere—thus reaching one-third of the nation's workforce at the time—the department did not do so on the basis of any specific findings of discrimination. Instead, department officials assumed that the rest of the nation was like Philadelphia—equally guilty of discrimination. What Nixon's first OFCC director, Arthur Fletcher, said when he announced the new Philadelphia Plan in June 1969 applied generally: there was a legacy of discrimination against minorities; this discrimination explained "obvious imbalances"; and "visible, measurable goals" were needed to "correct" them.[16] The OFCC's affirmative action thus aimed at correcting for "societal discrimination"—meaning, again, everything adverse that had happened to the shackled runner long before he got to the starting line.

The first Nixon term saw a second major advance for affirmative action. This involved the EEOC's effort, begun during the Johnson years, to define "broadly" the discrimination outlawed by Title VII. In 1971, the Supreme Court endorsed the commission's new definition of discrimination in *Griggs* v.

Duke Power Co.[17] Duke Power required a high school diploma or its equivalent for certain jobs at its power plant. Many fewer black than white applicants could meet this requirement, which the Court unanimously ruled was in violation of Title VII. In his opinion, Nixon's first Supreme Court appointee, Chief Justice Warren Burger, said that Title VII "proscribes not only overt discrimination but also practices that are fair in form but discriminatory in operation." By "discriminatory in operation," he meant practices that have an adverse impact upon minorities. Not even good intent, Burger wrote, could "redeem employment procedures or testing mechanisms that operate as 'built-in headwinds' for minority groups." Only if an employer could demonstrate "business necessity"—namely, that such procedures or mechanisms had a "manifest relationship" to the employment in question—could it avoid Title VII liability.

The *Griggs* decision threw into doubt every employment practice having a "disparate impact" upon minorities. Because of the potential liability, private employers now had to think about whether or not the percentage of minorities working in their companies mirrored the percentage of minorities in area labor forces. *Griggs* created enormous pressure to hire and promote by race and sex. This pressure would also be felt in 1972, when Congress extended the reach of Title VII to state and local governments.

The third advance during the Nixon years concerned the practice of setting aside a certain amount of federal business for minorities. In 1969, Nixon used an executive order to create an Office of Minority Business Enterprise (OMBE) within the Commerce Department, the purpose of which was to distribute $100 million to minority businesses. The office disclaimed making grants on the basis of race alone, but in fact the funds were set aside and went to minorities only. Nixon's evident enthusiasm for developing "black capitalism" could be seen in 1971 when those overseeing the distribution of funds told him their work was done and their function could be abolished. Nixon refused, writes historian Herbert Parmet, because "his interest in what they were doing was too great to let it go out of existence."[18]

The Nixon years saw the further articulation of just who would be eligible for affirmative action. As we have seen, the shackled runner in Johnson's Howard speech was black, and the original justification for affirmative action was remedial—to overcome the disabling effects of slavery and segregation, which blacks alone had endured. Soon, however, runners of other colors appeared alongside the black runners. In the late 1960s the reporting forms used by the EEOC in its enforcement of Title VII and the OFCC in its enforcement of the executive order sought from private employers information about the employment of not only blacks but also Hispanics, Asians, and American Indians. Under Nixon, the OFCC did not define the Asian category but did elaborate on who was Hispanic: "all persons of Mexican, Puerto Rican, Cuban or Spanish origin or ancestry." The Nixon order setting up the Minority Business Enterprise program defined an MBE as an enterprise "owned or controlled by one or more socially or economically disadvantaged persons"—"Negroes, Puerto Ricans, Spanish-speaking Americans, American Indians, Eskimos, and Aleuts." In 1973, the Small Business Administration issued regulations listing as socially or economically disadvantaged the following groups: blacks, American Indians, Spanish-Americans, Asian-Americans, and Puerto Ricans. Later, the agency added Eskimos and Aleuts.

As for women, their inclusion could not easily have been predicted. In the mid-1960s, politically active women were divided on the issue: some believed in protective legislation for women, others in an equal rights amendment. Very few pushed for affirmative action on the model of that being devised for blacks. But because Title VII outlawed employment discrimination on the basis of sex as well as race, the statistical approach to proving discrimination fashioned by the EEOC with respect to blacks was extended to women, making them candidates for numerical affirmative action. And because Executive Order 11246 was amended in 1967 to include women, affirmative action for them was also demanded from employers contracting with the government.

How and why the various programs included the groups they did has not been adequately explained, even by historians of public policy.[19] Even so, it is apparent from what we do know about this history that political considerations played a key role. In 1988, Herbert Hammerman, the chief of the EEOC's reports' unit during the commission's first years, wrote that in 1967 he urged removing Asians and American Indians from two new report forms because both groups were very small, there was no statistical evidence of discrimination against Asians, and American Indians who lived on reservations were not covered by Title VII while those who lived off reservations weren't readily identifiable. "No one disagreed," he said, "not even the [EEOC] chairman," who explained that he was unwilling to take the political heat that the removal would generate.[20] The Nixon administration's inclusion of Cubans in the OFCC's affirmative action enforcement seemed entirely a political gesture, since the relatively well-off Cubans fleeing the Castro regime were mostly Republicans.

By the early 1970s, many of the various runners lined up at the various starting lines of affirmative action could not claim their shackles resulted from slavery and segregation—or even that they were shackled. Differences both among and within the various racial and ethnic groups made the remedial rationale a weak frame for the expanding affirmative action edifice. Blacks had endured worse and more enduring discrimination than Hispanics, for example, and within the Hispanic category, Cubans had not experienced the harsh prejudice often faced by Mexican-Americans in the Southwest and Puerto Ricans in the Northeast. Hispanics, moreover, were not a racial group but an ethnic one whose members were of Spanish origin or culture. As for American Indians who were members of tribes, they had a unique relationship to the United States, the product of formal treaties; affirmative action for these Indians as well as the Alaskan natives with whom they were grouped as Native Americans seemed redundant, inasmuch as the members of these groups received special benefits because they belonged to "quasi-sovereign tribes." Women, meanwhile, were a quite different kind of affirmative action group. Constitutional law treated government classifications based on race and ethnicity differently from those based on sex. And while there had been laws excluding women from certain professions, and while there had been unequal pay for equal work done by women, women had not been forced to live among themselves, segregated from males. They lived intimately with males and by virtue of that fact were usually in the same social and economic classes as their male family members. Also, women, for a variety of reasons including personal choice, participated in the labor force at a rate less than half that for males.

Supporters of affirmative action typically defended the policy by dwelling on the unique history of blacks. In 1970, however, blacks comprised 11 percent of the population while those eligible for some form or other of affirmative action potentially included the majority of people living in the United States. The composition of this majority would be significantly altered through waves of immigration that the founders of affirmative action did not anticipate but which, by 1970, already had begun.

Admitting by Race

Affirmative action policies in higher education developed apart from the federal government, though with its blessing. Starting in the late 1960s, elite public and private colleges and universities devised new procedures for admitting blacks and other minority students in greater numbers than otherwise would have been possible under their usual academic standards. The most competitive professional and graduate schools did so as well. (Affirmative action plans that included women were found mainly in graduate schools.)

Much of higher education had previously maintained overtly discriminatory admissions policies against blacks, with some schools in the South dropping their policies only after Congress had passed the Civil Rights Act of 1964. But however they had treated blacks in the past, and in some cases because of the way they had, most institutions in all regions of the nation shared the belief that it fell to higher education to take a strong position on righting the nation's "one huge wrong," in Lyndon Johnson's words. As with employment, however, affirmative action admissions did not target blacks alone. The programs routinely included Mexican-Americans and other Hispanics, Asian-Americans, and American Indians.

It is in higher education that we see the emergence of the "diversity" rationale for affirmative action. The argument went as follows: There is "educational value" in a racially and ethnically diverse student body, because people "of color" enhance the learning environment by providing intellectual perspectives otherwise missing on campus. The diversity rationale was tied explicitly to numbers of minorities admitted: if there were too few admittees, they might become isolated on campus, their education might suffer, and their slight presence would not adequately enrich the educational experience available to all students.[21]

At least at the undergraduate level, there was no lack of schools where black and other minority students might be admitted under the same academic standards as all other students. Most likely, had there been no affirmative action, the same numbers of minority students would have been enrolled in undergraduate schools; only the distribution of students would have changed. As for the professional and graduate schools, the total number of minorities enrolled probably would have been lower, with the distribution of these students also altered. Most vigorously pursued by the better undergraduate schools and most graduate and professional schools, affirmative action thus was a policy that pulled minority students into schools otherwise beyond their reach. It was carried out on the understanding, perhaps best expressed by Alexander Heard, the chancellor of Vanderbilt University, that to treat minority students equally "we must treat them differently."[22]

The medical school at the University of California at Davis decided to treat minority applicants differently after it enrolled its first class in 1968. The school had no special admissions program for minority students, and the fifty students in that first class included no blacks, no Chicanos, no American Indians, and three Asians. Over the next two years, the school devised a special admissions program that admitted five blacks and three Chicanos in 1970 and, the class size having been doubled to one hundred, four blacks, nine Chicanos, and two Asians in 1971. Had the school not employed special admissions procedures, it would have admitted, under the standards applying to all other students, four Asians in 1970 and one black and eight Asians in 1971.

Because affirmative action admissions required preferential treatment on the basis of race and ethnicity, some non-minority applicants with better academic credentials were passed over in favor of minority applicants. Given the color-blind norms of the Civil Rights Act of 1964, the principal question facing higher education during these first years of affirmative action admissions was whether the programs ran afoul of the law. Like Title VII, which concerned employment, Title VI demanded nondiscrimination: "No person . . . shall, on the ground of race, color, or national origin, be excluded from participation in, be denied the benefits of, or be subjected to discrimination under any program or activity receiving federal financial assistance." Most institutions of higher education were covered by Title VI because they received federal funds. But the Department of Health, Education, and Welfare (HEW)—the agency enforcing Title VI— did not ask higher education to conform its new admissions policies to the law. Indeed, by the early 1970s, HEW had effectively rewritten Title VI by issuing regulations giving wide latitude to affirmative action admissions.

Triumph and Trouble in the 1970s

During the balance of the 1970s, affirmative action continued to gain ground, including vital legal ground in the Supreme Court.

In higher education, though the federal government was not going to intervene against race-based admissions policies, it was still possible that students who believed such policies had discriminated against them might bring a lawsuit. Moreover, a student challenging a race-based admissions policy at a state school might say that it violated not only Title VI but also the Fourteenth Amendment's equal protection clause, which applies to the states. In 1978 the Supreme Court decided this kind of case, a majority of five justices ruling in *Regents of the University of California* v. *Bakke* that neither the Constitution nor Title VI prohibits a university from taking race into account in its admissions procedures.[23]

In employment, the federal courts strengthened the disparate impact theory of discrimination. As a result, employers scrapped a wide range of recruitment, hiring, assignment, testing, seniority, promotion, discharge, and supervisory selection practices. Some employers resorted to "race-norming"— the practice of "adjusting" scores on ability tests judged free of cultural bias for differences among whites, blacks, Hispanics, and other groups to ensure racially proportionate results. Other employers ignored test results where necessary, hiring and promoting by the numbers in order to avoid litigation.

As for enforcement of the executive order, the Labor Department continued to extend the coverage, sweeping in banks, utilities, insurance and real estate companies, manufacturers, producers, and universities. From 1974 through the end of the decade, under Presidents Gerald Ford and Jimmy Carter, the department increased the regulatory pressure upon government contractors to hire minorities and women according to a barely veiled model of proportional representation. Under the elaborate process articulated in the executive-order regulations, a contractor had to compare its "utilization" of minorities or women in each "job group" with their "availability" in the area work force. If there were "deficiencies" in utilization, the contractor had to make up for them through affirmative action goals for hiring and promoting minorities and women and timetables to meet those goals. In 1977, Laurence Silberman, the former Labor Department lawyer who had defended the Philadelphia Plan against legal challenges, wrote in the *Wall Street Journal* that the executive-order enforcement inevitably drove contractors to employ preferences and even quotas.[24]

The critical legal question for affirmative action in employment was whether an employer could legally adopt preferences to avoid a Title VII lawsuit based on statistics or to satisfy the numerical demands of Labor Department bureaucrats. In 1979, in *United Steelworkers of America* v. *Weber,* the Supreme Court decided a case in which a private employer that contracted with the federal government had devised a racial quota for admission to a craft training program.[25] The threat of losing the federal contract and fear of liability under disparate impact theory had forced the employer "voluntarily" to adopt the quota. The plaintiff in the case—a white employee denied admission to the program on account of his race—claimed that the quota violated Title VII. Five justices, a majority, disagreed. The *Weber* decision removed any lingering doubt as to whether the courts would enforce the original, colorblind meaning of Title VII. Private and public employers alike now had a license to engage in preferential treatment and the discrimination it causes.

In regard to public contracting, in 1977 Congress passed and President Carter signed into law the Public Works Employment Act (PWEA). The law set aside at least 10 percent of the $4 billion appropriated under it for "minority business enterprises"—defined as enterprises owned by "Negroes, Spanish-speaking, Orientals, Indians, Eskimos, and Aleuts." The set-aside provision in the PWEA marked the entry of

Congress into the development of federal affirmative action policy, and it inspired states and localities to adopt similar programs. In 1980, in *Fullilove* v. *Klutznick*, the Supreme Court ruled, six to three, that the PWEA set-aside was constitutional.[26] There was no majority opinion, however, as the six justices who agreed on the result disagreed on the rationale for it. Nonetheless, the decision meant that the federal government had ample room to fashion race-based affirmative action programs in contracting, and in many other areas as well.

The Carter administration had argued for the decisions the Court reached in this trio of affirmative action cases. The administration's positions reflected the deepening commitment of the Democratic Party to racial preferences.[27] Meanwhile, opponents of preferences sought a voice in the increasingly conservative Republican Party. In Ronald Reagan's 1980 contest against President Carter, the former California governor campaigned explicitly against quotas. Reagan's opposition to the numerical devices associated with affirmative action brought to an end the era of bipartisanship in behalf of the policy, but did not bring the policy itself to an end. In fact, during the presidencies of Reagan and his Republican successor, George Bush, affirmative action managed in some ways to advance. And with the 1992 election of Bill Clinton and control of both the White House and Congress by the Democratic Party, it appeared that affirmative action's temporary license might never be revoked.

Yet two years later, with the election of a Republican Congress in 1994, the future of affirmative action suddenly became a subject of serious debate. Central to this debate, and to the choice we must make, is the path that affirmative action has traveled since the late 1970s. As we will see, higher education has continued to pursue preferences in admissions, sometimes even in defiance of the slight constraints placed on that practice by the Supreme Court. The Court has also continued its revision of Title VII by giving employers even more room to take race or sex into account—and thus to discriminate against those not of the right race or sex. And governments at all levels have pursued preferences in public contracting and other programs, even in the face of Supreme Court decisions imposing sharp constraints on government's ability to use race to apportion opportunity. Meanwhile, because of the substantial immigration of Hispanics and Asians, the population eligible for affirmative action has undergone enormous change, vitiating the policy's original remedial premise.

Each of these developments provides reasons for ending preferential affirmative action and recovering colorblind principles.

4

Remediation and Diversity: Affirmative Action in Higher Education

On July 20, 1995, the board of regents of the University of California voted to eliminate race as a criterion in student admissions, thus becoming the only institution of higher education to end preferential affirmative action. Ironically, the policy the regents retired was similar to one they once fought for in the courts—successfully. Indeed, it was the Supreme Court's 1978 decision in *Regents of the University of California* v. *Bakke* that ensured admissions by race in the California system and throughout American higher education.[1]

Today affirmative action in admissions is so well entrenched on so many campuses that it likely will require a determined outside force to end it. Even so, as the California regents who voted in the majority understood, the fact that a practice has won the hearts and minds of administrators and faculty does not make it right. There were good reasons to object to using race in admissions when the Supreme Court approved it in 1978. Today, there are even more.

Taking Race into Account

In 1972, Allan Bakke, a thirty-two-year-old mechanical engineer, applied for admission to the University of California at Davis Medical School. Despite excellent credentials, he was rejected. A year later, he applied again, with the same result. Both times his admissions prospects had been limited by a special program reserving 16 of the 100 places in each class for blacks, Chicanos, Asians, and Native Americans. Bakke, who is white, sued the university, contending that the program, which had admitted applicants with formal academic qualifications less impressive than his, had discriminated against him on account of his race. The Supreme Court ruled that the Davis program was illegal and ordered Bakke admitted. But the Court also said that the Davis medical school and institutions of higher education generally may take race into account in selecting students.

The Court did not express these conclusions in a majority opinion but in six separate opinions filling 156 pages. Four justices—Potter Stewart, Warren Burger, William Rehnquist, and John Paul Stevens—said that the Davis program unlawfully discriminated against Allan Bakke and ordered his admission. Four others—William Brennan, Byron White, Thurgood Marshall, and Harry Blackmun—said that the program was legal. The crucial opinion came from the pen of the ninth justice, Lewis Powell. Powell agreed with the conclusion of the first group, thus invalidating the Davis program and producing a majority of five votes for Bakke's admission. But Powell simultaneously agreed with the second group of four that an admissions office may "take race into account" in selecting applicants, thus producing another majority of five in favor of racial preferences. For Powell, a school may not do as Davis did—it may not use a two-track system that sets aside a fixed number of seats for minorities, insulating them from comparison with other students. Instead, it must use a presumably unitary admissions system that passes on all applicants regardless of race or ethnicity. In this kind of affirmative action program, Powell said, race may be taken into account as "a plus" that sometimes "tips the balance" in an applicant's favor.

The four justices endorsing the Davis program agreed with Powell on the critical question of whether a school may take race into account, while differing with him on just why a school may do that. For them, affirmative action was a remedy for "societal" discrimination, while for Powell it was a way of achieving "educational diversity." Their disagreement with Powell over the legality of the Davis program also concerned *how* race should be taken into account. "There is no difference," they wrote, between setting aside "a predetermined number of places" for minorities and "using minority status as a positive factor to be considered in evaluating [students'] applications." Powell said there was a difference: the kind of affirmative action program he endorsed would serve to protect the rights of people like Allan Bakke. It was the exclusionary nature of the Davis program that bothered him: only minorities won places under it. The Davis program, he wrote, "tells applicants who are not Negro, Asian or Chicano that they are totally excluded from a specific percentage of the seats in an entering class." Such applicants will know, he said, that "no matter how strong their qualifications . . . they are never afforded the chance to compete with applicants from the preferred groups for the special admissions seats." The right Powell said that Bakke had was, in effect, a right not to be excluded from the competition for all seats, a right to individualized or "competitive" comparison.

When the Supreme Court decided the *Bakke* case, there was much weeping and gnashing of teeth on the part of affirmative action supporters. New York City's *Amsterdam News* declared in a headline, "BAKKE—WE LOST." Columnist Tom Wicker of the *New York Times* wrote that "the validity and potential of affirmative-action programs may have been seriously, if not fatally, undermined." The national field director for the Southern Christian Leadership Conference was even more morbid, declaring that "the incentive to carry out affirmative action" had been "killed." The truth was different, as David Saxon, then the president of the University of California, immediately saw. He declared *Bakke* a "great victory." "Any ruling," he said, "that introduces restriction on the use of race is going to make it more difficult, but not very much more difficult."

Not very much more difficult, indeed. Powell envisioned an admissions system in which everyone receives "competitive" comparison and in which race is merely "a factor"—one among many. He argued that the applicant who loses out on the last available seat to another candidate "receiving a 'plus' on the basis of ethnic background will not have been foreclosed from all consideration for that seat simply because he was not the right color or had the wrong surname." In that event, he wrote, the student would discover merely that "his combined qualifications, which may have included similar nonobjective factors, did not outweigh those of the other applicant." Powell was deceiving himself. The student of the wrong race in Powell's example might not have been excluded from "all consideration" because of race, but he would have been excluded precisely from the seat he could have had but for his race. To license race as "a factor" is to license its use as the deciding factor.

Powell's opinion thus authorized racial discrimination in admissions. But in the years since *Bakke* was decided, some schools have even set aside the ostensible restriction on the use of race that Powell's opinion introduced—that is, the requirement that no admissions procedure be established that excludes applicants on account of race from "competitive comparison" with all other applicants. The University of Texas School of Law is an example. And for departing from Powell's opinion, which resulted in discrimination against Cheryl Hopwood, whom we met in chapter 1, the school drew little more than a slap on the wrist from the federal judge who heard her complaint.

Backsliding on Bakke

Cheryl Hopwood applied for admission to the University of Texas School of Law in 1992. She was rejected, even though her formal academic qualifications were superior to those of most of the blacks and Mexican-Americans admitted under an affirmative action program that was in key respects like the one Powell objected to in *Bakke.* In 1991, having used a single committee to process all applications since 1978—the year of the *Bakke* decision—the full admissions committee formed a subcommittee to process black and Mexican-American applicants only. As was true of the Davis medical school admissions procedures, the blacks and the Mexican-Americans evaluated by the subcommittee competed only among themselves for roughly 5 and 10 percent, respectively, of the 500 seats in the class. There was no single committee making "competitive" comparisons among all the applicants.

In 1994, on the eve of trial in the *Hopwood* case, the law school decided to do away with the separate admissions process it had used in 1992 (and continued in 1993 and 1994). In selecting students for the fall of 1995, the school decided to entrust all admissions decisions to one committee. It did so because, as a law school administrator explained during the trial, "when one gets sued in federal court, it catches one's attention." The scuttling of the separate-but-equal treatment came too late to spare the school an adverse judgment. Judge Sam Sparks invoked Powell's opinion in *Bakke* when he ruled against the separate admissions process. As he explained, "the constitutional infirmity" is that the procedure "fails to afford each individual applicant a comparison with the entire pool of applicants, not just those of the applicant's own race."[2] Of course, the lawyers who run the school were aware of the *Bakke* case. Indeed, for several years prior to 1978, the school's admissions committee had operated as two subcommittees, one passing on minority applicants and disadvantaged nonminority applicants, the other on everyone else. Though the admissions procedures differed from those used at the Davis medical school—there was no strict quota for minorities, and the committee considering minorities also evaluated and admitted some disadvantaged nonminorities— the school decided to scrap the dual approach in accordance with Powell's opinion in the *Bakke* case. In the *Hopwood* case, the school justified its backsliding on *Bakke* on the grounds that a separate admissions program would prove more efficient and effective. No doubt it did.

A few days after Judge Sparks ruled in the *Hopwood* case, the *Chronicle of Higher Education* tried to find out how many other schools had fallen away from the single-committee, individualized comparison approach endorsed by Powell in *Bakke*. "Most college officials said last week that they did not have formal policies resembling those at . . . Texas," the newspaper reported. "But many said privately that such policies were in use on an informal basis at a number of institutions."[3] The *Chronicle* went on to list instances of admissions procedures from the late 1980s and early 1990s that were at odds with Powell's *Bakke* opinion and which in some cases the U.S. Department of Education under President Bush had felt compelled to correct, or try to correct. Evidently, there are those in higher education who think they can defy Powell's opinion with impunity. Perhaps they understand that the four justices who endorsed the Davis program were right when they said there was no difference between affirmative action as Davis practiced it and as Powell said it should be practiced. Both approaches to affirmative action can admit roughly the same number of minorities. And both can discriminate against applicants not of the right race.

Though Judge Sparks told the Texas law school that its admissions procedures were unconstitutional, his ruling in the case wholeheartedly embraced the idea of what the school was trying to do, and he said it could admit by race so long as it did so according to Powell's *Bakke* opinion. Sparks, appointed to the bench by President Bush with the support of Senator Phil Gramm, said that the rights of Hopwood and three fellow plaintiffs had been violated, but he would not admit them because they could not prove they would have been accepted if the school had not discriminated against them—the judge put the burden of proof on them. Sparks awarded the plaintiffs a right they already possessed—that of reapplying for admission—and a single dollar in damages. Why so little? The school had not "intended to discriminate," he said. At least in the *Bakke* case, the person discriminated against by a similarly exclusionary admissions system was provided the remedy of admission. The backsliding on *Bakke* extends to the judicial system.

"We see Judge Sparks's opinion as a validation of the importance and propriety of our affirmative action program," said Texas law professor Sam Issacharoff, who added that the program will not change in any important respect. The school will take race into account, and it will count by race — it will keep its percentage goals. And so it will continue to discriminate against applicants like Cheryl Hopwood.

Remedying Discrimination

In his separate opinion in the *Bakke* case, Justice Blackmun wrote that "to treat some [minorities] equally, we must treat them differently." Different treatment has required, in Shelby Steele's words, "lowering . . . normal standards."[4] The record in the *Bakke* case shows how and why the Davis medical school decided to lower its standards for minorities. In 1967, when the school received applications for its first class, a single admissions committee measured every applicant by the same academic standard. As we saw in chapter 3, when this process resulted in the admission of three minority students, all of them Asian-Americans, out of a class of fifty, the administrators at Davis concluded that blacks, Chicanos, American Indians, and Asian-Americans could not perform equally with everyone else because of the depressing effects of societal discrimination.[5] To admit more minorities, the school decided to lower normal standards, setting up the separately administered special admissions program.

We can see what remedying the ill effects of discrimination meant in terms of lowered standards for the years Bakke applied and was rejected. In 1972, the average grade point average (GPA) of the regular admittees was 3.49, the special admittees 2.88. And the average GPA in the sciences of the regular admittees was 3.51, the special admittees 2.62. On the verbal section of the Medical College Admissions Test (MCAT), the average percentile in which the regular admittees scored was 81, the special admittees 46. The average percentile scores on the quantitative section were, respectively, 76 and 24. The respective figures for the two groups admitted in 1973 were similar. (As for Allan Bakke, 3.51 was his overall GPA, 3.45 for the sciences. And his percentile scores on the four sections of the MCAT were 96, 94, 97, and 72—considerably higher in each case than the average for the special admittees.)

The four justices who defended the Davis program had no trouble justifying it in terms of the remedial rationale the school offered. Typical of defenses of affirmative action at the time, their opinion focused exclusively on blacks. The argument they elaborated boiled down to this: There was slavery, and then there was segregation in the states in which most black Americans lived. Under slavery, the law imposed penal sanctions on anyone who tried to educate blacks. Under segregation, blacks were relegated to inferior schools. There was the *Brown* decision in 1954, but it was massively resisted, and racial discrimination in education, though ebbing, is still with us. The paucity of blacks who are doctors and who are now in medical school is a product of this long history of discrimination both generally and in education in particular. The discrimination has worked an adverse impact upon the academic performance of blacks, rendering them unable to qualify for medical school admission "under regular procedures." Departing from a "single admissions standard" and evaluating minorities under a different standard is an appropriate way of remedying the ill effects of discrimination.

This statement of the remedial argument is representative of how it was made two decades ago. Even then, its weaknesses were apparent. The most persuasive remedial argument holds that if A has injured B, then B has a justified moral claim against A, and A should do right by B. This argument is a moral argument that does not turn on race; in fact, it can be made apart from race. (Racial discrimination is one kind of injury; there are many others.) This was not, however, the remedial argument made in the *Bakke* case. In *Bakke*, the argument was that a school may remedy racial discrimination against Smith, a minority, and Smith's racial group (stretching back over the centuries) by admitting Smith even if that entails bumping aside better qualified persons not of the "right" race. The school need not have actually discriminated against Smith, and of course the Davis medical school hadn't discriminated against any minorities. This argument contemplated that institutions of higher education would assume a leading role in correcting for discrimination against minorities wherever and whenever committed. But because pursuit of this goal indeed meant that schools would discriminate against better qualified persons who themselves were not guilty of discrimination, it was hard to see then, as it is today, how this might constitute moral progress.

The remedial argument in *Bakke* also contained a dubious assumption—that discrimination mainly explains the academic performance of minorities. No one in 1978 should have been so foolish as to deny that discrimination can damage learning; no one should be so foolish as to deny this today. For a stretch of four years, from 1959 to 1963, Prince Edward County in Virginia shut down its public schools in an attempt to evade the desegregation requirements of the *Brown* decision. The fact that many of the county's black youth had no formal education during this period was without question educationally disabling. Even so, the admissions offices of higher education in the 1970s were not evaluating minority applicants who had all grown up in, metaphorically speaking, the Prince Edward County of the early 1960s. And precisely what explains educational outcomes (whether inferior or superior) in individual cases was then and remains today more complicated than the remedial rationale assumes. Students of race and ethnicity generally agree that discrimination is one of many variables that serve to explain educational (and other) outcomes.[6]

Since the *Bakke* decision, administrators and supporters of affirmative action have continued to offer the remedial argument, though not in the case of most Asian-American groups, since their academic performance leaves nothing to be overcome. (Today, most affirmative action admissions programs give preferences only to Filipinos, if they give preference to any Asians at all.) Sometimes the remedial argument changes in terms of detail. But always there is the same conclusion. In the *Hopwood* case, for example, the law school itself had had a discriminatory past (though it was quite distant), and Texas, unlike California, had been a slaveholding and later a Jim Crow state, complete with segregated educational systems. So the discrimination that the school's affirmative action program sought to remedy had a more specific articulation. But the basic thrust of the argument made by the Texas law school in the mid-1990s was the same one advanced twenty years earlier by the Davis medical school and articulated in the joint opinion by Justices Brennan, White, Marshall, and Blackmun. As Judge Sparks (in agreement with the law school) put it, "the legacy of the past has left residual effects that persist into the present" and which can be seen "in the diminished educational attainment of the present generation" of blacks and Mexican-Americans resident in the state of Texas. The educational attainment of these groups was such that the law school set the academic standard they had to meet for acceptance at a level lower than the one used to reject "white and other" applicants.[7]

The passage of years since *Bakke* has diluted the force of the remedial rationale. Most blacks seeking higher educational opportunities today attended first grade in the late 1970s or the early 1980s. And by the early 1980s, most formerly segregated school systems were officially desegregated. While American public education doesn't deliver as it should for students whatever their race or ethnic background, it is harder now than it was in the 1970s to explain "diminished educational attainment" mainly in terms of legally segregated schools.

At the same time, the practice of affirmative action today makes it difficult to accept the remedial rationale at face value. Until told by the federal courts in 1995 that its program was illegal, the University of Maryland administered a scholarship fund for black students only.[8] The university justified the program in terms of past discrimination—by the state. But the record in the case showed that in some years a majority of the black students awarded scholarships were from out of state. Likewise, in 1992, when Cheryl Hopwood tried to gain entry to the University of Texas Law School, the majority of blacks admitted under the school's affirmative action program, which was justified in terms of remedying that state's discrimination, were not Texas residents.

In their joint opinion in the *Bakke* case, Justices Brennan, White, Marshall, and Blackmun stated that affirmative action would help minorities who have suffered discrimination, indeed, who have been, as they put it, "isolated from the mainstream of American life." But today many, perhaps most, preferences in admissions are extended to minorities who are well ensconced in the mainstream, the offspring of middle- and upper-income parents.

Consider, for example, the case of Ron Chen, who was admitted to the Rutgers Law School in the early 1980s through its Minority Student Program (MSP). The mean LSAT score for MSP students is in the fiftieth percentile, as compared to a ninetieth percentile score for those admitted through the regular process. The MSP does not distinguish between poor and privileged minorities, operating on the premise that all minorities, regardless of their present station in life, have suffered from discrimination that has diminished their educational attainment. But note Chen's background. Both of his parents have Ph.D.s. He himself attended Exeter and Dartmouth. Chen cannot plausibly be portrayed as an "isolated" minority. In reality, it appears that Chen was held back less by any discrimination than by his own study habits. He told the *Washington Post* that he needed affirmative action to get into Rutgers because "I goofed off in college."[9]

The Lure of Diversity

Justice Powell was the father of the diversity argument. An institution of higher education, he said in his *Bakke* opinion, has the First Amendment freedom to make judgments about its educational mission. This freedom includes the latitude to select a student body, and the selection of a diverse student body can help promote the educational environment most conducive to "speculation, experiment, and creation" in which all students, minorities and nonminorities alike, benefit. By "diversity," Powell meant not mere racial diversity, but a broader diversity that results from a class made up of students of different races, geographic and cultural backgrounds, and special talents and abilities. Students bearing their diverse gifts enrich, he wrote, "the training of [a school's] student body and better equip its graduates to render with understanding their vital service to humanity." The intangible good known as educational diversity serves all students and also the larger society, and, for this reason, a school may take race into account as a potential "plus."

Powell approvingly appended to his opinion a summary of how the Harvard College admissions office conducted its effort. After choosing about 150 applicants on the basis of intellectual potential, the statement said, Harvard then filled out the rest of an entering class of more than 1100 on the basis of academic qualifications and *diversity*. Where once diversity meant students from different geographic regions, or football players, or potential stockbrokers, the statement explained, now it also meant "students from disadvantaged economic, racial, and ethnic groups." And they contribute what Powell implied: "something that a white person cannot offer." The statement said that the admissions office, in admitting minorities, had to pay "some attention to numbers," though it did not identify a figure or percentage. If there were too few minority students, it said, Harvard would not enjoy the full range of viewpoints that minorities possess. And the minorities themselves would feel "isolated" and therefore might not benefit from the Harvard educational experience.

The summary of the Harvard program admitted that "race has been a factor in some [of the school's] admissions decisions." But the summary did not say which races had been a factor, nor how much of a factor—how much of a "plus"—any particular race had been. Indeed, the Brennan opinion in the *Bakke* case observed that Harvard "does not . . . make public the extent" to which it uses preferences or "the precise work-

ings of its admissions procedures." The summary only suggested that the magnitude of the plus given for race or ethnicity is similar to that given for, say, an obscure hometown
or remarkable artistic ability. Powell himself tried to spell out
how much race might weigh, unhelpfully noting that the
weight given to race, like that given to other elements that
contribute to educational diversity, may "vary" from year to
year "depending upon the 'mix' both of the student body and
the applicants for the incoming class."

The diversity rationale as Powell laid it out had nothing to
do with remedying discrimination. It did not embrace the
claim at the heart of the latter rationale—that societal discrimination explains the academic performance of those
whom affirmative action prefers. Nonetheless, Powell offered
the diversity rationale in behalf of applicants who under the
academic standards applying to all others would not have
been able to obtain the educational opportunity they desired,
for there were no others it could have helped. Presumably,
affirmative action premised on diversity would admit most of
the same students as affirmative action based on remediation.

Powell's endorsement of the diversity rationale carried
weight in academe, and in the 1980s it began to appear in
arguments in behalf of preferential affirmative action in
employment and other contexts. But the rationale was flawed
when Powell offered it, and the passage of years has illu-
mined those flaws.

To begin with, Powell did not present the diversity rationale
in narrowly racial terms and, in fact, condemned diversity
defined in terms of "simple ethnic diversity." Instead, as he
elaborated the rationale, race was one among many items an
admissions office properly may regard as contributing to
"educational diversity." As we have seen, Powell invited institutions of higher education to do as Harvard College did in

pursuing educational diversity. But *Bakke* was a case about a professional school, not an undergraduate institution. Medical and law schools don't have bands or orchestras or football teams. Nor, for that matter, do graduate programs in physics or English. Powell's argument would have been more persuasive had he used as his model a professional or graduate school that was pursuing educational, as opposed to mere ethnic, diversity. Perhaps the reason he didn't was that no such models could be found. Today, professional schools cite Powell's opinion in pursuing affirmative action, but there is reason to believe that in most admissions offices Powell's educational diversity really means only racial and ethnic diversity. Consider again the *Hopwood* case. The University of Texas School of Law also justified its affirmative action program in terms of diversity, citing Powell, but race and ethnicity were the only diversity factors that warranted the kind of treatment they were accorded by the admissions office. No other "diversity" factor counted for as much as race did, in terms of overcoming disparities in index scores, nor in as many cases.

A second difficulty concerns an assumption found in the summary of the Harvard College admissions program, on which Powell relied so heavily—the assumption that minorities can bring to campus "something that a white person cannot offer." Harvard thus committed the cardinal error of affirmative action, which is to regard individuals as fungible members of their racial group. We need only turn to an intensive study of "diversity" on one of the most diversity-dedicated campuses in the Western world—the University of California at Berkeley—to see that not every minority admitted for diversity reasons brings to campus what he or she is supposed to bring. With no sense of irony, the faculty members who prepared the "final report" of the Diversity Project,

published in 1991, say that many of the Asian-American students they interviewed did not identify with the label "Asian-
American," and "several talked about having to *learn what it
means to be Asian American.*" The authors also interviewed
black students who they said "experience[d] a new kind of
pressure." As one reported, "I never felt any need to realize
my African-American descent and now I'm here, everybody
put such a stress and importance on it, I am realizing that I
am Black. . . . I never saw a colored world until I got here and
people started stressing the importance of color." The
authors also interviewed Chicanos who apparently did not
bring some distinctively minority perspective with them
when they enrolled as freshmen: "One undergraduate student . . . had no concept of what it meant to be Mexican—
even the word Chicano was new to her. Her arrival at the
Berkeley campus was described as 'a cultural shock' that she
eventually resolved after some difficulty."[10]

In 1995, Walter Dellinger, the assistant attorney general in
charge of the Office of Legal Counsel within the Justice
Department, sought to defend the logic of Powell's diversity
rationale by removing it from what he acknowledged was the
"racial stereotype" (found in the Harvard summary) which
presumes "that all individuals of a particular race or ethnic
background think and act alike." Rather, Dellinger said, the
diversity rationale may be premised "on what seems to be a
commonsense proposition that in the aggregate, increasing
the diversity of a student body is bound to make a difference
in the array of perspectives communicated at a university."[11]
But the truth of that proposition depends on the size of "the
aggregate." If the entire population of the United States were
enrolled at some university, no doubt that would be true,
notwithstanding that the campus would be unmanageable.
The smaller the "aggregate," the harder it is to say how

diverse the perspectives of the students in it will be, unless, of course, an admissions office has made a specific inquiry into the mind and character of *individual* applicants. But admissions offices practicing affirmative action do not routinely make inquiries into how each minority applicant thinks and what views he or she may hold—no more than it makes inquiries into whether each has been truly disadvantaged by discrimination.

Finally, the remedial rationale requires—at least in theory—that the group preferred by affirmative action also have experienced discrimination. By contrast, the diversity rationale as Powell explained it does not contain any such limiting principle. Diversity means what administrators want it to mean, and, of course, it facilitates discrimination against those applicants who do not meet the definition. It is in the name of diversity that some of the best schools in the nation today are rejecting applicants of Asian ancestry who are better qualified than other students they admit whose race or ethnicity (not Asian) is judged necessary for "diversity" purposes. In 1995, the University of California at Berkeley released information showing that if "diversity" had not been a criterion in admissions, the school would have admitted substantially more Asian-Americans. Thus one of the consummate ironies of affirmative action is that a group it once sought to help (Asians were originally included in the University of California at Davis Medical School's special admissions program) it now discriminates against. Such ironies can be explained, however, for rejecting race-blind admissions procedures necessarily means that race is something admissions officers can regulate. When guided by the diversity rationale, racial regulation today means discrimination against Asian-Americans. Tomorrow, it could mean discrimination against members of some other nonpreferred group.

Overcoming "Underrepresentation"

The four justices in *Bakke* who supported the Davis program occasionally used the term "minority underrepresentation." The term suggests that there is some norm of representation by which we can determine underrepresentation. The justices were coy, declining to say exactly what that norm is. They noted that the medical school at Davis reserved 16 percent of the seats in its classes for minorities, and they also noted that blacks and Chicanos alone constituted 22 percent of California's population. They took care, however, to say that their "allusion" to the latter figure was "not intended to establish either that figure or that population universe as a constitutional benchmark." Even so, the theory just below the surface of the opinion seemed to be one that assumed proportional representation by race in a world without discrimination. (Displaying a remarkable omniscience, the opinion also asserted that in a world without discrimination, Allan Bakke's academic qualifications would not have been good enough to gain him admission to the medical school.) The justices offered no evidence for this theory, perhaps because there can be none. "What is virtually impossible to know," writes economist Thomas Sowell, "are the patterns that would exist in a non-discriminatory world."[12]

Since *Bakke*, this difficulty has not troubled those dedicated to affirmative action in higher education, though few thoughtful defenders of the practice contend that the proportion of minorities in a college or professional school should simply reflect their proportion in the general population. Instead, they use a seemingly more plausible population group as the basis for comparison. For example, the percentage goals of 5 and 10 percent that the Texas law school set for, respectively, blacks and Mexican-Americans—the two groups that Texas officially designates as "underrepresented minorities"—were chosen because these were the percentages of blacks and Mexican-Americans being graduated annually from colleges and universities in the state.

But even this argument is suspect. Just because five percent of the college graduate population in the state of Texas is black does not mean that five percent must move on to law school. There is much to be known about the blacks who are college graduates before such a goal could begin to make sense—the quality of the school attended, the kind of degree obtained, the student's class ranking and career interest, and so on. Ultimately, the problem with proportionalism is that it treats groups, not individuals, and it is individuals who take tests, achieve grade point averages, choose colleges, majors, and careers—and who also may defy racial and ethnic classification.[13]

Like diversity, proportionalism is a recipe for discrimination—against members of groups deemed to be "overrepresented." And, of course, under this rationale too, it is not only whites but also Asians, as political scientist Harold Orlans has written, whom educational institutions believe "must have their overrepresentation reduced if other groups are to have their underrepresentation raised."[14]

The Great Experiment

Those officially designated as minorities for purposes of affirmative action have undergone what must feel like an ongoing experiment at the hands of higher education. Being treated differently in order to be treated equally—a "benign" act, according to advocates of affirmative action—has had its costs. Among them:

- *Doubts* on the part of affirmative action admittees about their abilities in comparison with other students. Among the general findings of the University of California at Berkeley "Diversity Project" was doubt among affirmative action beneficiaries as to whether they are *"bona fide* students." The lowered standards required by affirmative action tend to produce different ability levels in the student body. Berkeley has released information suggestive of the different academic standards it has used. In 1994, the mean Scholastic Aptitude Test (SAT) score for whites admitted was 1256, for Asians 1293, for Hispanics 1032, and for blacks 994.[15] At other exceptional state universities and elite private schools, the story is similar. For example, information compiled by the College Board and the University of Texas at Austin's Office of Institutional Studies shows that the average SAT score for whites entering the University of Texas in the fall of 1993 was 1147, for Asians 1155, for Hispanics 1043, and for blacks 991.[16] Standing alone, these numbers do not convey what we most need to know. Individuals are the ones who read and study and take tests, not groups, and it may well be that some persons who score "low" are nonetheless outstanding students. Even so, students admitted under affirmative action know their scores, and they know that without affirmative action they probably would not have been admitted to the schools in which they are now being educated. Under these circumstances, that some affirmative action admittees have doubts about whether they are "bona fide students" is not surprising, and so long as lower standards are used to admit certain students, such doubts will persist.

- *Unjust perception* of minority students by other students. Because affirmative action prefers individuals on the basis of their group membership, those minorities with academic credentials competitive with regularly admitted students may nonetheless be regarded with skepticism as affirmative action admittees. Writing in *The New Republic*, Yolanda Cruz, a biology professor at Oberlin College, tells a story about her first year in graduate school at the University of California at Berkeley. A second-year graduate student greeted her and said she had been looking forward to meeting the "twofer" who had been admitted that year. Because Cruz was a Filipino woman in a male-dominated field, and because affirmative action for Filipinos and women governed the admissions process, the second-year student had drawn the conclusion that Cruz was an affirmative action admittee, qualifying on two grounds. In fact, Cruz had been admitted on the basis of a sparkling academic record.[17]

- *Devaluing of academic credentials* gained by minorities. Where once a degree from one of the better schools plainly implied something about the academic achievement of the person who possessed it, the existence of affirmative action and the lower standards it requires provide a basis for employers to question that implication in the case of minority students. Whether the questioning is justified in the individual case is another matter, but the point is that to the extent people look at the degree, they will tend to perceive the bearers of those degrees in terms of how they believe the world of higher education works, thanks to affirmative action. In his 1995 book, *One by One from the Inside Out*, Glenn C. Loury makes the point succinctly: "The use of racial preferences can change the social meaning of black achievement by altering the inference that an external observer could logically make on the basis of observing it."[18]

- *Racial hostility* on campus. Smith College, Brown University, Colby College, and the Universities of Michigan and Wisconsin are among 175 schools reporting a rise in incidents of racist graffiti, jokes, anonymous hate notes, and brawls.[19] "The Diversity Project," published by the University of California at Berkeley explains this friction in terms of the "decrease in slots available to previously overrepresented majorities, and the increase in positions open to formerly underrepresented groups."[20] In other words, affirmative action is certainly a contributing factor to the rise in racial hostility, if not its cause.

The experiment minorities are undergoing has been producing a ripple effect of resentment. The year the University of Texas School of Law turned down Cheryl Hopwood, it passed over approximately 1,000 "white and other" applicants whose academic qualifications were equal to if not superior to those of the black and Mexican-American admittees. Though it is true that very few of the 1,000 would have been admitted under a colorblind system, it is nonetheless undeniable that absent affirmative action their odds of admission would have been somewhat better, though still long. Affirmative action thus is bound to breed resentment within a population far larger than those who actually experience discrimination at the hands of an admissions office committed to making decisions by race. The resentment is directed at affirmative action and perhaps also the institutions that practice it. It may also extend to those who are affirmative action's ostensible beneficiaries. If it does, the poison affirmative action is leaking into the body politic is potent indeed.[21]

The Practice of Affirmative Action

Since the late 1960s, enrollment of college-age black and Hispanic students—the most common objects of the affirmative action experiment today—has increased substantially. Enrollment steadily went up until the late 1970s. Then it declined a bit before picking back up slightly in the 1980s. Earlier in this decade, it reached historic highs. Preferential treatment played a role in these developments, but, as is true in other affirmative action contexts, we lack a reliable body of data showing how much of a "plus" race was in how many cases since the late 1960s. The little information in the public domain suggests that the more selective the school, the more race counted in admissions decisions.

Among the 1,400 undergraduate institutions annually rated by *U.S. News and World Report,* some 37 percent told the magazine in 1995 that they do not use race in their admissions decisions. Now as in the past, it appears that as a school becomes more selective, the more race counts as a "plus" in admissions. Given that the better schools enroll a small percentage of the total number of the nation's undergraduate students, it may be that most students (regardless of race) are attending colleges and universities where race matters very little, if at all, in admissions decisions.[22] Still, the substantial population of students that unsuccessfully seek entry to the more selective schools are naturally going to be interested in the procedures by which applicants win places. And most of the better schools are not only lowering normal standards to admit minorities but also showering them with scholarship money, sometimes regardless of need.

An example of an institution that will go to such great lengths to compete for minority students is the government department at Harvard University. The department receives as many as 700 applications for graduate school each year, admitting between 40 and 50 students. The department lowers its normal standards for minority applicants, judging them on whether it appears that they can complete the course. If this same standard were to apply to all applicants, some 200 to 300 students would be admitted. Once admitted, minority students are awarded scholarships "more lucrative than for all non-minority admits."[23] Thus does Harvard lower the standards and increase the money without regard for individual circumstances—an even more potent formula for unfairness.

Unending Affirmative Action

The most powerful argument for racial preferences in admissions (or anywhere else, for that matter) lies in the biography of someone who gained an opportunity, or a better opportunity, thanks to affirmative action, and has made so much of it that his or her achievements cannot in any way be questioned but are demonstrably first-rate, the equal of anyone else's. Some "affirmative action babies" have turned out to be non–affirmative action adults, persons who demand to be judged as individuals, on the same terms as anyone else, and whose work is truly excellent. If affirmative action in admissions continues, we can expect that some who benefit from affirmative action will ultimately transcend it.

But consider the costs. Whether schools practicing affirmative action follow Powell's opinion in *Bakke* or deviate from it, there will still be discrimination against those not of the right race, and those admitted under affirmative action still will be subjected to different standards—that is, lower standards. And because affirmative action necessarily makes race salient in our society, it will continue to provide a basis for those on campus as well as the larger public to think in racial terms not only about the students admitted under affirmative action, but also those whose race qualifies them for preferential treatment but whose academic qualifications make them competitive with anyone, regardless of race. Ironically, students admitted under affirmative action will continue to be stigmatized as unable to make it without preferences, even though most such students are by no means unqualified and would have gained entry to less selective schools—but honorably, on the same academic basis as all other students. After all, as we saw in chapter 1, the mean LSAT scores of the blacks and Mexican-Americans admitted to the University of Texas School of Law were high enough to suggest that they would have been able to gain admission to two-thirds of the nation's law schools.

Colorblind admissions procedures would bring an end to racial discrimination while withdrawing from the public the basis supplied by affirmative action for thinking and assessing in racial terms. Colorblind procedures do not promise to yield the more equal group outcomes that affirmative action was established in the first place to achieve. But then, that is not the ambition of colorblindness, which does not strive to engineer socioeconomic outcomes, but instead demands that we treat all persons as individuals, without regard to race.

In his opinion in the *Bakke* case, Justice Blackmun famously wrote: "To get beyond racism, we must first take account of race. There is no other way." Blackmun said he yielded to no one in his earnest hope that the time for what he clearly regarded as an absolute necessity would end, that affirmative action would be "only a relic of the past." "At some time," he said, "beyond any period of what some would claim is only transitional inequality, the United States must and will reach a stage of maturity where action along this line is no longer necessary. Then persons will be regarded as persons, and discrimination of the type we address today will be an ugly feature of history that is instructive but that is behind us."

The problem that Blackmun did not foresee is that it is not so easy to turn on and off the use of race. The remedial rationale that he endorsed in the *Bakke* case implies an end to affirmative action, for a remedy may be put away once it has worked its effects. But the years since *Bakke* was decided have demonstrated how hard it is for higher education to quit taking account of race. Indeed, the "diversity" and "underrepresentation" rationales often cited by education officials today provide a basis for unending affirmative action. After all, the racial and ethnic mix of our society is always changing, thanks to demographic factors, and, for the same reasons, some group will always be "underrepresented," just as some other— alas for its members—will always be "overrepresented."

If we are going to reach that stage of maturity where persons are regarded as persons, we are going to have to quit thinking and counting in terms of race. There is no other way.

5

Counting and Norming: Affirmative Action in the Workplace

Title VII of the Civil Rights Act of 1964, as amended in 1972, prohibits employment discrimination in both the private and public sectors. Some 94 million Americans work for employers covered by the law. Three million of these workers toil for the federal government, and 16 million draw paychecks from local and state governments. The remaining 75 million Americans work for private employers, roughly a third of whom are contractors with the federal government and are covered by Lyndon Johnson's Executive Order 11246, which requires affirmative action.[1]

When it enacted Title VII, Congress thought it was creating a right that Americans would enjoy, regardless of skin color or sex—the right to be free of race or sex discrimination in the workplace. But the push for numerical affirmative action in employment has deformed Title VII. Today, the statute cannot be relied upon to stop the discrimination that is committed in the name of affirmative action. That is the bad news, but there is worse: judges are being asked to ignore the statute's core requirement of nondiscrimination in order to allow employers to discriminate against employees in order to achieve workplace "diversity." If this view of Title VII prevails, any of the 94 million Americans protected by the statute—blacks, whites, Hispanics, Asians, men, women—could be at risk.

Brian Weber's Wrong Race

As we saw in chapter 3, the 1979 case of *United Steelworkers of America* v. *Weber* legalized developments in affirmative action begun in the late 1960s.[2] It is imperative for us to look at that case more closely, for it was in *Weber* that the Court began carving out exceptions to the nondiscrimination principle at the core of Title VII.

In 1968, a young man named Brian Weber went to work for Kaiser Aluminum at its plant in Gramercy, Louisiana, twenty-five miles up the Mississippi River from New Orleans. Six years later, when the plant announced that it was offering nine on-the-job training opportunities for skilled craft jobs—those of instrument repairman, electrician, and general repairman—Weber applied but was not chosen. As he soon discovered, a racial quota had bumped him aside. Under a collective bargaining agreement between Kaiser and its union, the plant had agreed to enroll in the craft training program one black applicant for every white applicant until the percentage of blacks employed in its craft positions was the same as that of blacks in the Gramercy labor force, which happened to be 39 percent. Workers were eligible to enter the program based on their seniority, and because whites tended to have worked more years, the Gramercy plant created separate seniority lists for blacks and whites and then picked from each list on an alternating basis. The scheme enabled the plant to secure the quota of at least 50 percent black enrollment, as the nine workers selected for the program included five blacks and four whites. Two of the blacks had less seniority than Weber, who is white.

Weber decided to sue, believing that the law was squarely on his side. Title VII not only made it unlawful for an employer to classify his employees "in any way which would deprive or tend to deprive any individual of employment opportunities . . . because of such individual's race, color, religion, sex, or national origin," but also included a provision that seemed to speak precisely to Weber's situation: "It shall be an unlawful employment practice for any employer, labor organization, or joint labor-management committee controlling apprenticeship or other training or retraining, including on-the-job training programs, to discriminate against any individual because of his race, color, religion, sex, or national origin in admission to, or employment in, any program established to provide apprenticeship or other training."

Weber won in the federal district court and then withstood an appeal to the Fifth Circuit Court of Appeals. But when the case went to the Supreme Court in 1979, Weber lost. Writing for the majority, Justice William Brennan acknowledged that the question before the Court was whether Title VII *forbids* private employers and unions from voluntarily agreeing" to use "affirmative action plans that accord racial preferences," and he concluded that Title VII did not condemn Kaiser's quota.[3] Brennan said that Weber's argument rested upon a "literal" interpretation of Title VII and was "not without force." But it was wrong, he said, because Title VII had to be interpreted not in terms of its actual language, but by examining its legislative history and "historical context." Brennan spun out the following argument: in passing Title VII, Congress was mainly concerned with improving the economic plight of blacks. Therefore, Congress could not have intended to prohibit private employers from "taking effective steps" to accomplish this goal. Accordingly, the provisions in Title VII that Weber cited "cannot be interpreted as an absolute prohibition against all private, voluntary, race-conscious affirmative action efforts to hasten the elimination" of the vestiges of the past.

To reach this result, Brennan had no choice but to reject the actual words of Title VII. As he acknowledged, the statute clearly prohibited discrimination "because of race" in hiring and in the selection of apprentices for training programs. Moreover, the "legislative history" that Brennan used to trump the statute's words was a selective reading of Congress's intent in passing Title VII. As Justice William Rehnquist, in dissent, showed in his exhaustive treatment of the legislative history, Congress can have intended only what Title VII actually said. Congressional opponents of the statute argued that under its terms the federal government might well interpret it as requiring unwilling employers to achieve racial balance by granting preferences to minorities. Supporters responded that the law could not be interpreted that way because it not only does not require preferential treatment, it does not even permit it. Title VII thus outlawed all discrimination "because of race"—including, as Rehnquist pointed out, that which results from "affirmative action plans that accord racial preferences."

Brennan repeatedly stated that the issue in the case involved merely a *voluntary* affirmative action plan undertaken by a *private* employer. But *Weber* meant far more than Brennan let on. Kaiser, a federal contractor, was under pressure from the Labor Department to increase minority representation in the crafts, and it feared a Title VII disparate impact lawsuit citing the low numbers of black craft workers. (This was hardly an empty fear; in its friend-of-the-court brief in the case, the federal government said that "voluntary" preferences had to be allowed under Title VII since the Court had held in the 1971 *Griggs* case that unequal group outcomes might violate the law.) As Kaiser's lawyers told the Supreme Court, "voluntary action may in reality be a misnomer, for legal compulsion was present as surely as if a suit had been filed or a contract lost."[4] The *Weber* case thus was not about a private employer acting purely on its own, voluntarily, but about a private employer operating within a federal legal environment that nudged and pushed it toward racial preferences. The decision limited the reach of Title VII's nondiscrimination principle in order to affirm the validity of this public environment and the preferential affirmative action it all but required.

In the years prior to the *Weber* decision, lower courts had sometimes imposed quotas on guilty defendants, acting on authority explicitly provided by Title VII to remedy proven violations of the nondiscrimination clauses by ordering "affirmative action." Because Title VII did not define remedial affirmative action in terms of quotas or preferences, the judicially ordered numerical remedies constituted a departure from the statute's colorblind norms. Judges typically justified the remedies in terms of necessity, contending that there was no other way to force change upon discriminatory employers. In *Weber*, of course, the Court was not deciding whether Kaiser had actually discriminated against blacks. But the Court knew that Kaiser thought it could face a Title VII lawsuit alleging unequal group outcomes. So the Court might have rationalized its decision to permit "voluntary" affirmative action in terms of the "arguable violation" theory: an employer believing such a lawsuit is imminent may lawfully prevent it by assuming guilt and establishing preferences to secure more equal group results. Had the Court taken this approach, it would have maintained affirmative action as a remedy for discrimination still tied to the employer's conduct —though the link now would be assumed and not demonstrated. While the Court did not say so, the problem with this rationale for "voluntary" affirmative action was that it was not roomy enough to include the numerical affirmative action imposed on federal contractors by the Labor Department. For as we saw in chapter 3, while the Labor Department justified its first affirmative action plans in terms of discrimination in the Philadelphia construction industry, the department did not bother thereafter to produce specific findings of discrimination as it imposed affirmative action on construction contractors in other cities and then on nonconstruction contractors throughout the nation. Instead, the department justified affirmative action in terms of overcoming generalized or societal discrimination, which explained a contractor's "underutilization" of minorities or women as compared with their "availability." Brennan in effect embraced this rationale when he spoke of the need to remedy "racial imbalances" that were the result of traditional patterns of segregation. The *Weber* decision thus provided legal doctrine large enough to support what were then the boldest forms of affirmative action in the workplace.

The ruling, however, was a deceptive one. Brennan spoke warmly of entrepreneurial liberty and expressed aversion to government regulation. In one sense, of course, Brennan did deregulate business by lifting from it the burden of strict nondiscrimination, the essential command of Title VII. But he did this in order to enable businesses lawfully to adopt the affirmative action that the government required. The decision transformed Kaiser, in effect, into a public utility subject to affirmative action regulation. The decision was hedged about with qualifications, such as one stating that preferences shouldn't be used to maintain balances but only to eliminate imbalances. Indeed, one could read the decision thinking that most of the nondiscrimination principle was still in force, that discrimination against anyone was still unacceptable, permissible against whites only in special circumstances and then subject to various controls. But this was not the case. The decision allowed discrimination against whites so long as it was committed in pursuit of affirmative action in behalf of blacks (and other minorities). Such discrimination need not be justified in terms of the employer's own discriminatory conduct. And the affirmative action the decision authorized extended only incidentally to persons an employer might have discriminated against (and of course the employer might have discriminated against no one). The point of the affirmative action was not to remedy actual wrongs against identifiable persons but to benefit persons of the race experiencing societal discrimination. *Weber* thus treated individuals not on their own terms but as members of racial groups. The result was at odds with what the authors of Title VII intended, but it was demanded by affirmative action.

Discrimination Under Reagan

Ronald Reagan's appointees in the Justice Department knew what *Weber* had wrought. Late in 1981, Reagan's assistant attorney general for civil rights, William Bradford Reynolds, said bluntly that *Weber* had been "wrongly decided." But despite the administration's outspoken opposition to quotas, no legislation was sought to reverse the decision. While the Reagan and Bush administrations did manage to constrain the use of preferences in some contexts, the real story of those twelve years was the persistence and expansion of affirmative action in employment, through which Title VII experienced a further deformation.[5]

The Reagan administration could have changed the Labor Department's enforcement of numerical affirmative action upon government contractors. After all, the executive order was not a statute of Congress, and the regulations implementing it were entirely the handiwork of officials ultimately reporting to the president. But though the Labor Department reduced the paperwork burden on contractors, it continued to require them to adopt preferential "goals and timetables," which inevitably cause discrimination.

In 1985, for example, the Reagan Labor Department cited the United Bridge Company of Lenexa, Kansas, for failure "to exert adequate good faith efforts to achieve the minimum minority utilization goal of 12.7 percent for Truck Drivers and the minimum female utilization goal of 6.9 percent for Carpenters, Heavy Equipment Operators, Iron Workers, Truck Drivers, and Laborer Trades." The requirement imposed on the company, four of whose fifteen employees were minorities, and which used only one or two truck drivers on the job at any one time, was that it must "recruit and hire qualified

minorities and females until such time as the required utilization goals have been met. Should no qualified minorities
and females be available, the company will document its
efforts to meet its goals for the trades." The company thus
could not hire a better-qualified person if a minority or
female were available. It was encouraged if not effectively
required to discriminate, since the loss of government business was the ultimate sanction.

Early in Reagan's second term, Attorney General Edwin
Meese III decided that the discrimination caused by the
executive-order enforcement should be ended. Leading a
group of Cabinet-level appointees that included Communications Director Patrick Buchanan and Education Secretary
William Bennett, Meese pushed for legal changes that would
have prevented the Labor Department from requiring or
encouraging preferences based on race or sex. But Labor
Secretary Bill Brock prevailed against the Meese-led effort,
saying that although nonpreferential policies were desirable,
he was not yet ready to endorse them.[6] Meese ultimately concluded that it was unwise to push the president to act, for he
feared that the Democratic Congress might pass a new
statute reinstating the regulatory scheme altered by a new
executive order or new regulations, and that Reagan then
would be drawn into a legislative fight of uncertain outcome
that could weaken him and the Republican Party as well.

One reason Brock maintained Labor's preferential policy
is that many private employers had grown accustomed to the
deal struck by the *Weber* decision. So long as the regulatory
burden was not excessive, those who contracted with the federal government were willing to hire and promote by the
numbers that Labor's compliance officers might suggest,
especially since having the "right" numbers of minorities and
women in their workforces also helped insulate them from

Title VII lawsuits. The pro-preference legal environment also led to the full employment of "human resource" specialists, devotees of numerical affirmative action. Their growing presence in the private sector meant that affirmative action there would be hard to uproot. Whether pushed by necessity or genuine belief, heads of the largest corporations said that affirmative action was "good for business," meaning that it improved a company's relationship with the community it served. In 1985, 88 percent of the 197 corporations responding to a *Fortune* magazine survey of the Fortune 500 said they would maintain quotas even if they were not legally required to do so. The title of the magazine article reporting the survey results was "Businessmen Like to Hire by the Numbers."[7]

In 1987, the Supreme Court was again asked to interpret Title VII in a voluntary affirmative action case, this time involving a public employer. At issue in *Johnson* v. *Transportation Agency* was an action taken pursuant to an affirmative action plan adopted in 1978 by the transit agency of Santa Clara County in California.[8] Under the plan, the percentage of minorities and women in the agency's workforce was to mirror that found in the Santa Clara workforce. Even more, the percentage of minorities and women in each job category was to reflect the percentage of minorities and women holding that kind of job in the Santa Clara area. Setting both long-term and short-term goals, the agency's plan authorized those making hiring and promotion decisions to consider "as one factor" the race or sex of a "qualified" applicant.[9] The plan, in many ways similar to those widely used in the private sector, thus obscured the fact that race and sex would be the deciding factors as employers pursued their goals.

The transit agency wound up in a lawsuit as a result of a hiring decision. Seeking to fill a vacancy for road dispatcher — a job no women then held — the agency winnowed the list of nine qualified applicants to two employees, Diane Joyce and Paul Johnson. One panel, and then another, interviewed both, and Johnson, who had higher scores for both the written test and the interview, was recommended for the job. But the agency's affirmative action coordinator told the director that Joyce should get the job, and the director agreed. Johnson sued, charging that the county had violated Title VII by denying him a job opportunity because of his sex. The district court sided with him, finding that he was "more qualified" for the position and that Joyce's gender was "the determining factor" in the director's decision to choose her over him. "But for [Johnson's] sex, male, he would have been promoted," wrote the court. And "but for Diane Joyce's sex, female, she would not have been appointed."

But like Brian Weber eight years earlier, Paul Johnson lost in the Supreme Court, with Justice Brennan again writing the majority opinion. The six-to-three decision implied an expansion of the rationale for affirmative action. In *Weber*, the Court had said that an employer may use preferences to remedy imbalances caused by societal discrimination, meaning the discrimination against blacks that historically had taken many forms, including denying blacks the opportunity to acquire craft skills. In *Johnson*, the Court ruled that an employer voluntarily may use preferences to overcome "underrepresentation" in terms of race or sex. But the Court did not tie "underrepresentation" to societal discrimination; it did not say that the former was caused by the latter. The upshot was that an employer now could use preferences merely to overcome "underrepresentation," whatever its cause. As the legal scholar Herman Belz has written, "employers were now free to create a balanced work force," and they "had more latitude to achieve that end than courts did in their broad remedial power."[10]

In a candid concurring opinion, Justice Stevens conceded that the Court had interpreted Title VII "in a fundamentally different way" from the "absolute blanket prohibition against discrimination" that it contained, which neither required nor permitted preferences for members of any group. For unknown reasons Stevens did not participate in the *Weber* case. But he was unwilling in *Johnson* to call upon the Court to reconsider an interpretation of Title VII that he knew was "fundamentally" at odds with what Congress had intended.

Affirmative Action Exposed

By the late 1980s, affirmative action encountered problems of its own creation. These stemmed from the disparate impact approach to alleging discrimination on the part of an employer that the Supreme Court had blessed in its 1971 *Griggs* decision.

In the first disparate impact cases, in the 1970s, the plaintiffs typically had argued that particular employment practices were responsible for unequal group outcomes. But in the 1980s some plaintiffs started pointing to disparities without bothering to cite particular employment practices. This approach had some logic, for as we have seen, affirmative action in the 1980s had developed into an instrument not only for remedying societal discrimination, regardless of whether an employer had committed discrimination, but also for overcoming underrepresentation, whatever its causes. But in 1989 the Supreme Court said that statistics alone are not enough. In *Wards Cove* v. *Atonio,* the Court made clear that plaintiffs in disparate impact cases must identify the actual employment practices they think are responsible for the unequal results.[11]

The Court said this in a case in which the plaintiffs had persuaded the Ninth Circuit Court of Appeals that Alaskan salmon canneries could be sued under the disparate impact approach because they employed mainly whites in skilled jobs and mainly nonwhites in unskilled jobs. Significantly, the Court also ruled that this type of comparison is the wrong one, insisting that the right one must be between "the racial composition of the qualified persons in the labor market and the persons holding at-issue jobs."

Had the Court upheld the Ninth Circuit, employers would have been even more vulnerable to disparate impact litigation, and thus even more inclined to resort to preferences. As Justice Byron White explained in his opinion for the Court, approving the approach urged by the plaintiffs "would mean that any employer who had a segment of his work force that was—for some reason—racially imbalanced could be hauled into court and forced to engage in the expensive and time-consuming task of defending the 'business necessity' of the methods used to select the other members of his work force. The only practicable option for many employers will be to adopt racial quotas, insuring that no portion of his work force deviates in racial composition from the other portions thereof; this is a result that Congress expressly rejected in drafting Title VII."

The facts and interpretations of law that came to the Court in *Wards Cove* persuaded a majority of the justices that disparate impact litigation had gone off the rails. The Court used the case to address other issues in disparate impact cases. These included which party should shoulder the burden of proof, and also what evidence might justify a challenged employment practice. Some students of the Court thought that the *Wards Cove* decision might spell the beginning of the end of the disparate impact doctrine, a product, as we saw in chapter 3, of federal bureaucrats and judges. In this view, the Court would take additional cases in order to recover Title VII's original meaning—that of a statute that outlaws disparate *treatment,* not disparate *impact.*

The civil rights lobby was not pleased with *Wards Cove.* It went to Capitol Hill in search of new law, and after two years of fierce battle between the administration and the Democratic Congress, President Bush signed the Civil Rights Act of 1991. The legislation left unchanged some of the key parts of *Wards Cove* and even strengthened the requirement that the plaintiff identify particular employment practices responsible for the disparate outcomes. As for the most contested part of the act—the provision dealing with what may justify an allegedly discriminatory employment practice—its impact is unclear. The lower courts have had few opportunities to interpret and apply it.

The civil rights lobby was pleased with the new law, and they had reason to be, if only because it codified the disparate impact approach. Congress, the branch of the federal government closest to the people, had finally signed on to what is in fact a dubious understanding of discrimination. Information about the number of minorities (or nonminorities, for that matter) hired for a certain job is relevant under Title VII to an inquiry into whether purposeful discrimination has taken place. But low numbers shouldn't create a presumption of discrimination on the part of the employer strong enough to put him in the dock, as the disparate impact approach maintains. For even when the kind of statistical comparison that the Court sanctioned in *Wards Cove* is made, it does not follow that the remaining statistical differences between or among racial groups can be attributed to racial discrimination, whether on the employer's part or even that of society in general. Age, area of residence, and years of

schooling, among other variables, are also part of the explanation. Census Bureau data show, for example, that the median
age for non-Hispanic whites is 35.5, 28.6 for blacks, and 25.8
for Hispanics; the older people are the more work experience
they have, and thus they tend to hold better jobs. Argument
against the disparate impact approach, however, was seldom
heard in the congressional debate over the new law.

The 1991 law also saved affirmative action from itself, for
it outlawed "race-norming"—the practice of adjusting scores
on employment tests for differences among racial and ethnic
groups. Under this practice, blacks had been graded on a
curve with other blacks, whites with whites, Hispanics with
Hispanics, and so forth. A member of one group did not compete directly with those of the other groups.

Race-norming had become widespread during the 1970s
thanks to the Court's endorsement of the disparate impact
approach. Even so, the practice was little known outside of
personnel offices, and what had escaped public notice
entirely until late 1989 was that the U.S. government itself
was engaging in race-norming. Since the start of the Reagan
administration, the Labor Department had encouraged state
employment services to administer its job skills test—the
General Aptitude Test Battery (GATB)—and to race-norm the
scores before referring test-takers to private employers.
Some forty states using the test had done as Labor coun-
seled, with the number of tests being normed climbing into
the millions every year. There had been no question about
the predictive validity of the GATB, which is used in screen-
ing applicants for semiskilled electrical and blue-collar jobs,
and measures reading, vocabulary, math, dexterity, and other
skills. Indeed, the National Academy of Sciences had found
it was not biased against minorities. But those taking the test

didn't know the games being played with their scores. Officials converted the raw scores of the test takers to percentile ranks within each of three groups—blacks, Hispanics, and others. Thus, a black, a Hispanic, and a white achieving the same raw score of 300 (in one example based on the Labor Department's conversion score table) were given the race-normed scores of 83, 67, and 45, respectively.

Once these facts entered the public domain in early 1990, race-norming could not survive. The process of measuring certain skills had been corrupted and test-takers deceived in order to facilitate preferential treatment for blacks and Hispanics and "benign" discrimination against whites (which category also included Asians). The whole business suggested that blacks and Hispanics could not compete equally with whites and Asians and instead must be assigned to their own playing fields if they are to score and win. At the same time, it degraded the achievements of blacks and Hispanics whose raw scores were equal to or better than those of any other test takers.

Race-norming survived for as long as it did only by dwelling in obscurity and deception, where it enjoyed the support of affirmative action advocates. But though the 1991 law prohibited race-norming, it did not dismantle the legal regime that had given rise to it. Indeed, by legislating disparate impact theory, the law ensured that private employers might have to find other, if less efficient, means for making sure that their work forces divide out into the "right" numbers by race.

The fact that race-norming had been the fashion for so long should have provided an opportunity to judge the aspiration of those who decided in the late 1960s that it was necessary to define Title VII discrimination "broadly," in terms of disparate impact. As noted in chapter 3, the social engineers

of racial equality thought they could accomplish their goal by taking what amounted to a shortcut. In their effort to improve the socioeconomic condition of minorities, they thought they could reduce the problem of equality to an issue of discrimination—so long, of course, as they could define discrimination not in the traditional terms of bad intent, but in terms of any conduct that adversely affected a minority group, a point that they would make statistically. In conceiving the issue in these terms, the engineers of equality flouted what students of race and ethnicity could have told them: namely, that socioeconomic outcomes for various groups cannot be reduced to a matter of discrimination but have far more complicated explanations, found in education, family structure, and the like. The engineers of equality took what one of them, the EEOC's Alfred Blumrosen, called "the optimistic view of the racial problem in our nation" in which "we are in control of our own history."[12] This was Great Society talk, the product of an era of overweening confidence in the power of government to produce rapid socioeconomic change. Two decades later, the "optimistic view" had resulted in the repugnant and deceitful practice of race-norming. The better choice lay in focusing private and public policies on what Blumrosen called the "difficult" areas of education and family relations, where progress may come "only gradually," as he put it, but surely not artificially.

Ironically, the reduction of the pursuit of racial equality to racial discrimination and the disparate impact approach it necessitated may have impeded educational progress by minorities. While minorities have made educational advances over the past three decades, they might have registered more gains but for the disincentives to achievement that can be attributed to disparate impact litigation. In 1995, the *New York Times* reported that researchers studying the hiring practices

of American businesses were concerned that "employers seem to pay no attention to the grades and performance of high school students" and that "if employers do not care, why should students?" Among other reasons the article cited to explain the employers' lack of interest in academic performance was fear of a disparate impact lawsuit if a company demanded educational credentials on the part of high school graduates seeking jobs.[13]

Discrimination in the Name of Diversity

Though private employers say they fear lawsuits, they also say, as we have seen, that they "like to hire by the numbers." In recent years many of them have been doing so on the basis of "diversity," a trend also evident in the public sector.

As we saw in chapter 4, diversity differs from remediation in some key respects. Remediation looks to the past and seeks to overcome the effects of past discrimination. It is in theory limited in duration, for once the ill effects of discrimination are remedied, affirmative action no longer is needed. Diversity, on the other hand, has nothing to do with the past. It does not presume that its beneficiaries are disabled; it does not regard (or insult) them as shackled runners. Instead, diversity regards all of us as just fine the way we are. Our virtue is our diversity, our races. Directly contradicting the traditional civil rights idea that race ought to be irrelevant to how people treat each other, diversity holds that we should encourage race-based judgments, for race is meritorious in itself. Diversity-based affirmative action thus promises to be perpetual.

In the world of work, diversity can mean many different things; it's like an empty suitcase, awaiting whatever clothes might be thrown in. In the context of private employment, for example, diversity can mean having Hispanic employees to serve Hispanic customers. In the context of a police department, it can mean having a cohort of officers who reflect the community and, it is hoped, increase the effectiveness of the force. Whatever diversity is said to mean in a given setting, however, it always means using race or ethnicity (or sex) in allocating limited opportunities—and thus discriminating against someone who offers insufficient "diversity."

A lawsuit filed in the early 1990s illustrates this point exactly. It also suggests how Title VII might undergo its next deformation.

The case involves Sharon Taxman, whom we met in chapter 1. Taxman taught in the business education department at Piscataway High School in New Jersey. Facing a decline in students in that unit in 1989, the school board decided to lay off one of its ten teachers and narrowed its choice to two equally qualified teachers who had the least seniority—Taxman, who is white, and Debra Williams, who is black. As it happened, the two had taught exactly the same length of time, having begun their employment on the same day in 1981. In the past, the school board had broken seniority ties through a random process, such as drawing lots. All such ties, however, had involved two persons of the same race. In this case, the board decided not to use a random method because of the uncertainty of the outcome. It wanted to retain Williams, because otherwise there would have been no black teachers in the business education unit. Presumably, the board might have told Taxman, bluntly, that because she is white, she was out of a job. But the board had at hand its own affirmative action plan, adopted in 1975 and revised in 1983, which provides that "when candidates appear to be of equal qualification, candidates meeting the criteria of the affirmative action program will be recommended." Those favored persons are the minorities that the New Jersey State Department of Education so designates—blacks, Hispanics, Asian-Americans, and Native Americans. Thus by invoking its affirmative action plan to break the tie, the board knew it could retain Williams and terminate Taxman. So the deed was done. The news was broken to Taxman in a letter that spoke the typically roundabout language of affirmative action: "The board of education has decided on its commitment to affirmative action as a means of breaking the tie in seniority entitlement."

Taxman complained to the Equal Employment Opportunity Commission. The EEOC investigated and forwarded her complaint to the Justice Department. In 1992, the final year of the Bush administration, the department sued the school board, charging it with a violation of Title VII. In response, the department claimed to have acted according to a voluntary affirmative action plan and told the judge that it wanted the case decided according to the standards set forth in *Weber* and *Johnson*. But it turned out that the board had not adopted its plan to remedy its own discriminatory practices (there had been none) or those generally of society, as *Weber* requires. Nor was the purpose of the plan to overcome a manifest racial imbalance, as *Johnson* requires. The truth was that the school system employed more minority professionals than their representation statewide or in Middlesex County, its immediate locale. If Debra Williams had been let go, the decision would not have resulted in "underrepresentation" of blacks among Piscataway public school teachers. Her retention would have "maintained" the racial balance of the business education unit, but both *Weber* and *Johnson* said that an employer may not use preferences to do that.

In other words, even the loose standards of the Supreme Court's Title VII decisions governing voluntary affirmative action were not an adequate defense for the decision to let Taxman go. Shifting course, the board, in language reflecting the spirit of the age, told the district court that its layoff decision was justified in terms of "racial diversity." That is, the board wanted a faculty that would reflect the racial diversity of the community and the student population, even in a teaching unit as small as its business education department.

This diversity rationale went beyond the Supreme Court's rulings, and Judge Mary Trump Barry was unwilling to carve out new law on her own authority. "The Board has cited no authority that has been willing to stray so far from the holdings of *Weber* and *Johnson*," she wrote in her 1994 decision in the case, "and this court will decline the invitation to do so." Judge Barry ruled that the board's decision to lay off Taxman violated Title VII. Taxman, like Williams, she wrote, had "a legitimate entitlement to have the layoff decision made randomly rather than on the basis of race."[14]

The decision in the *Taxman* case shows that there is something of the nondiscrimination principle still alive in Title VII. But after winning in Judge Barry's court, the Clinton Justice Department, which had inherited and continued the case, decided on appeal that its position in the case had been wrong. The Clinton reversal shocked most Justice Department observers, both because it left Sharon Taxman high and dry and because no one could recall a case in which a new Justice Department, having continued a case brought by its predecessor and won it, then decided to change the government's position once the decision was appealed. Then, too, there was the fact that the case involved a layoff, and whatever the Supreme Court has said about preferences in other employment contexts, it has consistently frowned upon using race to decide whether people keep or lose jobs they already have. Withdrawing as the plaintiff in the case in July 1994,

the Clinton Justice Department two months later filed in the
Third Circuit Court of Appeals a friend-of-the-court brief in
support of the Piscataway school board. The brief explained
why the federal courts should stray from the holdings of
Weber and *Johnson*—and thus further from the original
meaning of Title VII—and permit still more discrimination.

The Justice Department's position was this: the Supreme
Court spelled out the permissible bases for voluntary affirmative action in *Weber* and *Johnson,* but the Court did not
declare those bases the only ones. Because it did not, we
must entertain the possibility that voluntary affirmative
action may be justified even in deciding layoff questions for
reasons other than remedying societal discrimination or
overcoming underrepresentation. And there are various
opinions by five members of the Supreme Court indicating
that diversity, especially in the context of education, is an
acceptable basis for voluntary affirmative action. Though no
majority of the Court has ever said this (and some of the
justices cited are no longer on the bench), we think this is
what a majority would say if it were asked—maybe in this
case.

The Clinton Justice Department showed some brass in
this argument, though it disingenuously said it was only
reading the law as it existed, not trying to create new law. The
Justice brief quoted a passage by Justice Brennan in the
Weber case—"We need not today define in detail the line of
demarcation between permissible and impermissible affirmative action plans"—that it took as an invitation to try to
advance the law. The department did so by subordinating the
original meaning of Title VII to what the Supreme Court had
said about it, and by reasoning that because it could find no
case squarely against what the school board had done, then
the board's action was lawful. "There is no case that anyone

can point to that clearly says they did violate . . . Title VII,"
said Assistant Attorney General Deval Patrick, in congressional testimony in 1995.

While the brief signed by Patrick assured the public that
Piscataway presents "a narrow issue" because the case
involves merely a layoff decision between two equally qualified employees, the brief also explicitly declined to take a
position on whether diversity may justify a preference when
the choice is between persons of unequal qualifications. If
that is the next case, there is no reason to think that the
administration would fail to ask a court to read Title VII to
allow diversity-based discrimination in this far more common situation. After all, the Supreme Court has never explicitly ruled against such a proposition.

Breaking new ground, Patrick's brief yielded a surprise for
those who think of diversity in terms of "traditionally segregated" or "underrepresented" groups. As the brief explained,
"diversity" doesn't favor one race over another but must be
viewed "in the circumstances." "Potentially, the same interest
in faculty diversity could tip the balance in favor of a white
teacher if the composition of a department would otherwise
have included no white teacher."

President Clinton agreed with this understanding. "As
long as [the rationale] runs both ways, or all ways," he said
during a press conference in October 1994, "I support that
decision. That is, [if] there are other conditions in which . . .
there were only one white teacher on the faculty in a certain
area, and there were two teachers [who] were equally qualified, and the school board . . . decided to keep the white
teacher also to preserve racial diversity." To spell out what
Clinton implied, "keep the white teacher" means "lay off the
black teacher because the black teacher is black." It could

mean laying off a Hispanic teacher because the Hispanic teacher is Hispanic. And so on.

The Clinton administration thus would transform Title VII into a statute that has strayed so far from its original meaning as to efface it almost completely. For Title VII, so transformed, would permit discrimination for the sake of a diversity that employers have ample discretion to define and that encourages people to believe, contrary to what the law originally taught, that there are important differences among the races and that these differences should be the basis for employment decisions.

No Problem

In March 1995, the Labor Department released an in-house report on "reverse discrimination" cases from 1990 to 1994.[15] The report, prepared by old affirmative action hand Alfred Blumrosen, found that these cases constituted between one and three percent of all discrimination cases and that "a high proportion" of the claims in these cases were "without merit." The report was flawed: there were both more reverse discrimination cases than Blumrosen found—inexplicably, he missed the *Piscataway* case—and more that were successful. Still, Blumrosen was right to say that reverse discrimination constitutes a very small percentage of all discrimination cases. The problem lay in his conclusion. "This research," he wrote, "suggests that the problem of 'reverse discrimination' is not widespread."

His research does not suggest this. Under Title VII, deformed as it now is, employers have broad latitude to discriminate in order to remedy past societal discrimination and to correct manifest imbalances. Precisely because the law is tilted against a successful lawsuit, the paucity of cases from 1990 to 1994 doesn't say anything about the extent of the problem of "reverse discrimination." We don't know how much discrimination results from affirmative action in the workplace, just as we don't know the extent to which employers engage in preferential treatment.[16] What we do know is the state of the law. And if the diversity rationale wins acceptance in the federal courts and spreads beyond the "narrow" context endorsed by the Clinton administration, we can be confident that there will be fewer "reverse discrimination" cases for the next Blumrosen to report—assuming anyone is still interested. The only difference will be that not just whites but individuals of all races will be unprotected. As President Clinton unwittingly confirmed, diversity is an equal opportunity discriminator.

6

Stacking the Deck:
Affirmative Action in Contracting

Thomas Stewart of Spokane, Washington, owns a company that builds guardrails and signs for highways. But since Stewart is a white male, his skin color and his sex routinely work against him. Even when he is the low bidder on projects funded by the federal government, he still stands to lose if the company he's competing against is owned by women or by members of certain minority groups. Not long ago, he got a familiar rejection letter from the owner of Mid Columbia Paving. "You were low on this project," he was told, "but, again, we were caught in the minority goal trap."[1] In other words, under government rules, Mid Columbia, the general contractor on a federally funded highway project, had to give the subcontract to a higher-bidding minority company.

Today the nation is awash with programs that use race or sex (or both) as a criterion in awarding public contracts. Sponsored by governments at all levels—local, state, and federal—the programs vary in form. Some "set aside" a portion of contracting business for firms owned by minorities or women. Others allow everyone regardless of race or sex to compete but award the business to minorities or women so long as their bid isn't a certain percentage—typically 10 percent—more than the low bidder's. This is called a "bid preference"—a term that disguises the real preference, which is race- or sex-based. What the programs have in common, of course, is that they discriminate on the basis of race and sex.

There is a good reason to oppose affirmative action in contracting that has nothing to do with its use of race and sex to distribute opportunity. It is, simply, that citizens deserve economy in government, and "set-asides," "bid preferences," and the like unnecessarily increase the price of government. For example, the Defense Department's inspector general reported last year that contracts for long-distance services awarded under affirmative action to minority-owned businesses over an eight-month period in 1992 cost taxpayers an extra $1.1 million.[2] This economic objection to affirmative action in contracting, however, has seldom persuaded those in charge of the governmental bodies that have created and sustained them. Politicians often have responded to less refined but more politically powerful forces—the demands of constituents for "their" piece of the public pie.

In recent years, the Supreme Court has handed down rulings that express deep skepticism about the use of race on the part of government. But affirmative action in public contracting (as well as other public programs) has survived. Some jurisdictions have ignored the Court. Others have recast their programs to avoid or at least postpone legal difficulties. In some cases, the discrimination these jurisdictions practice is not so obvious, but, paradoxically, that may make the problem worse, since covert discrimination can be harder to reach and expose. If the Court someday finds itself having to perform the judicial equivalent of laser surgery to reach well-insulated sources of discrimination, it will have itself at least partly to blame. The growth of affirmative action in government contracting and other programs can be traced to the 1980 case of *Fullilove* v. *Klutznick.*[3]

"A Fair Share of the Action"

As we saw in chapter 3, the Small Business Administration created the first program for awarding government contracts on the basis of race. The year was 1968, and it was in response to the riots in Watts and other urban areas that the SBA decided to use its discretionary authority to set aside federal contracts for small businesses owned by "socially or economically disadvantaged individuals"—another bit of affirmative action newspeak, since the business was being reserved for only black individuals. Soon enough, Congress showed that it liked the idea of minority set-asides when it enacted the Public Works Employment Act (PWEA) of 1977. The legislation authorized spending $4 billion on local public works projects, the idea being to stimulate a sluggish economy. Included in the PWEA was a provision requiring each prime contractor to subcontract at least 10 percent of the dollar value of the work to "minority business enterprises" (MBEs). In essence, the PWEA subsidized local procurement and ordered localities through the MBE provision to implement a minority set-aside.

This provision implied a departure from standard contracting procedures, for the longstanding rule was that, all other things being equal, the low bidder on a contract wins. Under the new law, an MBE didn't have to be the low bidder to land the job—although his price could not be "unreasonable." The PWEA defined an MBE as a business that was at least 50 percent owned by minority group members or, if it was publicly owned, 51 percent of whose stock was held by minorities. And the statute left no doubt who those minorities could be. It named the eligible groups: "Negroes, Spanish-speaking, Orientals, Indians, Eskimos, and Aleuts."

Not since 1854 had Congress passed a statute that explicitly identified its beneficiaries in terms of race or ethnicity.[4] For this reason, one might think that the legislation was passed only after a vigorous debate over the wisdom of passing a law classifying Americans on the basis of race. That didn't happen. Representative Parren Mitchell, the Maryland Democrat and head of the Congressional Black Caucus, offered the MBE provision in the House as a floor amendment. There were no committee hearings on the provision, no reports. The amendment passed by voice vote. In the Senate the story of casual adoption was much the same.

According to the scant legislative history of the provision, its supporters presented it as a way of ensuring that minority businesses would benefit from a government procurement program. In 1976, Mitchell said, minority-owned businesses had won less than one percent of all federal procurement while minorities made up between 15 and 18 percent of the general population. "All [the set-aside] attempts to do," he said, "is to provide that those who are in minority businesses get a fair share of the action from this public works legislation." They hadn't been able to get their fair share in the past, Mitchell and his colleagues said, because the intricacies of the bidding process were perplexing and getting financing was difficult. And then, too, there was racial discrimination, which the provision's supporters said could be seen in the low rates of participation in procurement by minority businesses. The purpose of the set-aside, said Mitchell, was to redress a longstanding grievance.

Challenged on constitutional grounds, the MBE provision was upheld in *Fullilove*. Chief Justice Warren Burger, who wrote the plurality opinion, swallowed whole the remedial rhetoric, even though Congress had not identified any specific wrongdoing. No member of Congress said that a contracting officer at the federal, state, or local level had ever discriminated against a minority business. Nor did any member of Congress offer evidence alleging discriminatory behavior on the part of prime contractors—the ones who would be obligated to subcontract 10 percent to minority businesses. Again, the evidence Mitchell and his colleagues offered took the form of statistical disparities. Their argument was, basically, that there had been societal discrimination against blacks, that this discrimination explains their low rates of participation in procurement programs, and that the MBE provision would remedy the discrimination. It did not matter to Congress that the set-aside, in remedying discrimination practiced by no one in particular, would benefit minority businesses regardless of whether or not they had actually experienced discrimination in procurement—indeed, regardless of whether they even existed prior to the PWEA. All that mattered was their race.

Congress engaged in no deep reflection when it targeted other minority groups for the set-aside. There is nothing in the statute or its legislative history explaining why these groups as opposed to some others were "owed" the remedy. As it happened, Congress simply used the list of groups that the SBA had added to its set-aside program during the 1970s. And in 1977, the SBA's list of "socially or economically disadvantaged groups" included "American Indians, Spanish-

Americans, Oriental Americans, Eskimos, and Aleuts." The SBA had devised this list without hearings or formal findings, but that fact didn't concern Congress when it borrowed the list, or the Court when it reviewed the legality of the MBE provision.

As for the 10 percent figure for the set-aside, Congress chose it arbitrarily. Justice Lewis Powell, in his concurring opinion, obtusely explained why he found it appropriate: it fell "roughly halfway between the present percentage of minority contractors [4 percent] and the percentage of minority group members in the Nation [17 percent]."

Fullilove did not produce a majority opinion. Six justices agreed that the MBE provision was constitutional while differing on the reasons for that conclusion. But nothing the six justices said promised to constrain the federal government's use of race. The decision signaled to Congress and the executive branch that the federal government could continue at full speed down the set-aside path. And though *Fullilove* concerned a federal program, state and local jurisdictions took inspiration from it, crafting similar set-asides.

Reining in the Use of Race

Nine years after the *Fullilove* decision—plenty of time for affirmative action in contracting to take root and grow at all levels of government—one of the local programs finally wound up in the Supreme Court. At issue in *City of Richmond* v. *J. R. Croson Co.* was a set-aside adopted by the city council of Richmond, Virginia, in the spring of 1983.[5] The program had *Fullilove* written all over it. During the hearing in which the council approved the measure, the city's purchasing director, having reviewed construction contracts let by the city for the

five years prior to 1983, said that only two-thirds of one percent had been awarded to minority-owned businesses even
though minorities made up more than 50 percent of the
Richmond population.[6] Parren Mitchell had made the same
kind of comparison when he recommended the MBE provision. Evidently, *Fullilove* persuaded the supporters of the
ordinance that they didn't need to do much more than cite
the same kind of disparity. "I'm not saying that we have discriminated in any individual case in the past," said the city
attorney during the hearing. "What we're saying is [that]
there are statistics about the number of minorities that were
awarded contracts in the past which would justify the remedial aspects of the legislation."[7] The city council decided to
"remedy" this societal discrimination by picking for the
amount of business to be set aside a percentage, as Justice
Powell, a native Richmonder, might have done, "roughly
halfway" between two-thirds of one percent and 50 percent.
Thus, the council specified that 30 percent of all public
works contracts were to be subcontracted to minority-owned
businesses. Even though Richmond's non-black minorities
constituted less than 2 percent of the city's population, the
groups that the council designated for set-aside business
were essentially the same ones found in the MBE provision
upheld in *Fullilove* — "Blacks, Spanish-speaking, Orientals,
Eskimos, or Aleuts."[8]

Understandably, supporters of the Richmond set-aside
thought it stood a pretty good chance of winning approval in
the Supreme Court. But by a vote of six to three, the Court
found the program unconstitutional.

The decision marked a major development in constitutional
law. The Court relied on the equal protection clause of the
Fourteenth Amendment. The provision obligates the states,
and thus a local government like Richmond, not to "deny to

any person within its jurisdiction the equal protection of the laws," and, in the 1940s and 1950s, the Court made clear that the federal government also has the same duty. In reviewing equal protection challenges to racial classifications, the Court by the 1970s had decided that they must meet "strict scrutiny." That is, race-based measures are unconstitutional unless "narrowly tailored" to achieve "a compelling state interest." By that time, too, it was clear that no government of any kind could legally discriminate against blacks or other minorities; racial classifications of the "invidious" kind could never survive strict scrutiny.

But with the advent of affirmative action, the question arose as to whether racial preferences sponsored by government must also meet strict scrutiny. In the 1978 *Bakke* case, discussed in chapter 4, Justice William Brennan wrote an opinion joined by three other justices contending that racial preferences are "benign racial classifications" and therefore should be reviewed under the more relaxed standard of "intermediate scrutiny": the government interest need only be important and the racial classification need only be "substantially related" to its achievement. The Court did not resolve this doctrinal issue in the *Fullilove* case, but began to do so in *Croson*. For it was in *Croson* that, for the first time ever, a majority of the Court said that racial preferences—at least those adopted by state and local governments—must meet strict scrutiny. To state the decision simply, there are not two equal protection clauses, one for minorities and one for nonminorities, but just one, for persons of all races. Regardless of your race, the Court said, if you are claiming that a state or local law has deprived you of your constitutional right to equal protection on account of race, and that law does in fact contain a racial classification, we must review your claim in terms of strict scrutiny, the highest standard there is.

Applying strict scrutiny to the case at hand, Justice Sandra Day O'Connor wrote for the majority that racial classifications must be "strictly reserved for remedial settings," suggesting that remedying discrimination is the *only* interest the Court would regard as "compelling." But, continued O'Connor, Richmond had failed to provide "a strong basis in evidence" for the discrimination that its set-aside ostensibly remedied. None of the items the city offered as evidence — including the statistical disparity — were strong enough to permit an inference of discrimination. Thus, the city lacked a "compelling interest" for "apportioning public contracting opportunities on the basis of race." And as for the set-aside itself, it was not a "narrowly tailored remedy" — even assuming there was discrimination to be remedied. The city council hadn't considered race-neutral means of increasing minority business participation in city contracting but instead immediately resorted to the 30 percent set-aside. Further, the set-aside did not include terms that would enable administrators to determine whether those benefiting from it had actually suffered discrimination at the hands of the city or prime contractors. Race — and only race — mattered. And while the black-majority city council, governing a city more than half black, had passed an ordinance with blacks in mind, the set-aside included other groups for whom, O'Connor said, there was "absolutely no evidence" of any kind of discrimination they might have suffered in the Richmond construction industry. O'Connor made it clear that a race-based remedy can't be just for any group. "Narrow tailoring" at least means that if a group is getting a remedy, it must also be a group that's been discriminated against. O'Connor pointed out that the ordinance, under which any eligible firm anywhere in the country could get the city's business, could lead to bizarre results. "A successful black, Hispanic, or Oriental entrepreneur" from some other part of the nation could enjoy "an absolute preference over other citizens [in Richmond] based solely on their race," she wrote.

Croson suggested that the Court had watched with growing alarm the often casual adoption of racial preferences by governments throughout the nation. *Croson* was clearest about the constitutional obligations of states and localities. Presumably, the federal government was under the same constraints. But in the 1990 case of *Metro Broadcasting, Inc.* v. *Federal Communications Commission*, the Court approved racial preferences used by the FCC in the grant and transfer of broadcast licenses—preferences mandated by Congress not in response to any discrimination on the part of the commission or the broadcast industry but in an effort to increase the representation of blacks, Hispanics, Asians, and Native Americans (thereby ensuring a "diversity" of minority viewpoints) in the communications sector.[9] The four justices who had argued for intermediate scrutiny in the *Bakke* case— which concerned a *state* program—finally saw their view prevail within the Court, as Justice Stevens (who had dissented in *Fullilove* and voted with the majority in *Croson*) joined them to form a majority of five. Radiating confidence about the capacity of government to regulate on the basis of race to good effect, this majority explained that it is possible for government to distinguish between "benign" and "invidious" racial classifications, and that the benign ones—benign because they mean no harm to minorities and only incidentally burden nonminorities—shouldn't be subject to the same harsh review as the invidious ones.

The four dissenting justices sharply disagreed in an opinion written by Justice O'Connor. There is no such thing as a benign racial classification, she said, observing that "to the person denied an opportunity or right based on race, the

classification is hardly benign." For this reason, all racial classifications must satisfy strict scrutiny. Referring to the compelling interest that government must demonstrate under
strict scrutiny, O'Connor noted that "modern equal protection doctrine has recognized only one such interest: remedying the effects of racial discrimination." The FCC policies fell
short on this score, she said, because they were justified in
terms of promoting broadcast diversity—an objective "too
amorphous, too insubstantial, and too unrelated to any legitimate basis for employing racial classifications."

Though *Croson* and *Metro Broadcasting* involved different
levels of government, the real issues dividing the Court were
which *level* of review that racial preferences adopted by any
government should trigger and whether, to borrow O'Connor's words, equal protection doctrine should recognize any
compelling interest other than remedying discrimination. As
it happened, *Metro Broadcasting* did not remain "good law"
for very long. The majority in the case was the last one that
Justice William Brennan was able to piece together before
retiring. And the next year saw the retirement of Brennan's
most constant voting companion, Justice Thurgood Marshall.
President George Bush got the chance to fill both vacancies.
The four dissenters in *Metro Broadcasting*—Justices O'Connor, Rehnquist, Scalia, and Kennedy—needed to pick up
only one of the Bush appointees, David Souter and Clarence
Thomas, in order to overrule the legal doctrine in *Metro
Broadcasting*. Their moment arrived in 1995, as Thomas
joined the dissenters to overturn *Metro Broadcasting* in the
case of *Adarand Constructors* v. *Pena*.[10]

In chapter 1, we met Randy Pech, the owner of Adarand
Constructors, which specializes in building guardrails for
highways. Pech, who is white, sought to become a subcontractor on a federal highway job. Mountain Gravel and Con-

struction was the prime contractor on the project. Adarand submitted the low bid, but Mountain Gravel instead chose Hispanic-owned Gonzales Construction. The federal government paid Mountain Gravel to make that choice. Congress appropriates money for highway projects, and the U.S. Transportation Department awards the prime contracts. Federal law devised during the 1980s requires that agencies' prime contracts include a "subcontracting compensation clause." The clause promises the prime contractor a bonus if it hires subcontractors certified as small businesses controlled by "socially and economically disadvantaged persons"—blacks, Hispanics, Native Americans, and Asians, among others. The prime contract awarded to Mountain Gravel contained a subcontracting compensation clause promising a bonus of approximately 10 percent. By choosing the higher-bidding Gonzales over Adarand, the owners of Mountain Gravel pocketed a bonus of about $10,000 on the $100,000 subcontract.

Randy Pech challenged the color line that the subcontracting compensation clause embraced. By encouraging the racial preference, he said, the federal government had violated his constitutional right to the equal protection of the laws. Pech lost in the lower courts, which were obligated to apply the "intermediate scrutiny" standard of *Metro Broadcasting*. But the Supreme Court gave him another chance to prevail when it held that that standard is the wrong one.

Writing for the Court, Justice O'Connor ruled, in effect, that there is only one Constitution. It does not matter whether you are white or black, minority or nonminority, and it does not matter whether you think a state government or the federal government has violated your constitutional right to the equal protection of the laws, and it does not matter whether the race-based measure is the "invidious" kind of the Jim Crow era or the "benign" type supporters of affirmative action say it is. Citing the statements of Justice Harlan and others who endorsed colorblind law, O'Connor said that the Constitution requires that any government's race-based measure must be subjected to the most demanding standard of review—strict scrutiny. "Any person, of whatever race," she wrote, "has the right to demand that any governmental actor subject to the Constitution justify any racial classification subjecting that person to unequal treatment under the strictest judicial scrutiny. . . . All racial classifications, imposed by whatever federal, state, or local governmental actor, must be analyzed by a reviewing court under strict scrutiny."

The Court thereupon sent Pech's case back to the lower courts, with instructions to look at the case again, but this time using the strict scrutiny standard. *Adarand* completes the clarification in constitutional law that *Croson* initiated and which *Metro Broadcasting* put in doubt. Together, the *Croson* and *Adarand* decisions mark a renewal of the great tradition of colorblind law. The tough standards the Court has set forth apply broadly to all government programs, not just contracting. Yet it's not surprising that both *Croson* and *Adarand* involved contracting, for that is an area in which preferential treatment has so plainly corrupted the constitutional duty to govern impartially. Unfortunately, there has been substantial resistance to the standards the Court has set forth.

Resistance in the States

In the *Croson* case some 234 state and local governments joined a friend-of-the-court brief advising the Court to uphold Richmond's set-aside. These jurisdictions also had been using race in contracting, and they had adopted their programs with about as much thought and care as the Richmond city council had displayed when it passed the ordinance the Court found unconstitutional. After *Croson*, several dozen jurisdictions found their programs wanting when measured by strict scrutiny, and decided to end them. But the overwhelming majority of jurisdictions either refashioned their programs to make them less vulnerable to a lawsuit or kept them unchanged, deciding to defend them only if challenged in court.

Thanks to the *Adarand* decision, states and localities may have one less argument in defense of their use of race in the allocation of contracts. This is the argument that "the federal government made us do it": we receive federal grants for transportation projects; the grants come with strings of affirmative action attached; and, under the Supreme Court's decisions in *Fullilove* and *Metro Broadcasting*, the courts should defer to Congress and therefore decline to strike down the affirmative action programs we have established to please the folks in Washington.

Soon after the Court issued its ruling in *Adarand*, a California state judge rejected this argument. The case involved an affirmative action program administered by the Los Angeles County Metropolitan Transportation Authority, which set aside 29 percent of its construction work for firms owned by minorities or women. Federal money mixed with local money underwrote a subway construction project that Michael Cornelius, a tunnel engineer, had bid on as a subcontractor. Cornelius would have landed the job but for his race—he is white. Seeking to meet its 29 percent goal, the transit authority decided that the prime contractor on the project needed to steer more work to minorities and women. The state court judge found the transit authority's affirmative action plan unconstitutional and, invoking *Adarand*, disposed of the notion that the plan was legal because it reflected federal requirements.[11]

Adarand thus may limit the defense states and localities can make in behalf of affirmative action in contracting. But consider how dedicated to preferences many of these jurisdictions have been since the Court's decision in *Croson*. In that case, the Court did not say government may never use racial preferences, but it did make resort to preferences almost impossible. In her majority opinion, Justice O'Connor said that Richmond's "reliance on the disparity between the number of prime contracts awarded to minority firms and the minority population of the city" is "misplaced," observing that the kind of disparity that might pass muster would be one "between the number of qualified minority contractors willing and able to perform a particular service and the number of such contractors actually engaged by the locality or the locality's prime contractors." O'Connor made plain, however, that this disparity, even when properly drawn, must be "statistically significant." And even then it could provide only "an inference of discriminatory exclusion"—such exclusion being the only condition, it appears, to which a racial preference might be the right response.[12] Still, under O'Connor's opinion, even before a jurisdiction could entertain the idea of using preferences, it would have to find out more about any such exclusion. Among other things, it would have to ask who was responsible for the exclusion and whether it might be corrected through race-neutral means.

A reasonable response to *Croson* and the enormous difficulty of inferring discrimination from disparities would be to get out of the business of apportioning contracts on the basis of race. But since 1989, more than one hundred state and local jurisdictions have commissioned "disparity studies" to sustain or expand their programs. George R. LaNoue of the University of Maryland Graduate School, one of the foremost authorities on the arcane subject of disparity studies, points out that the "research" often is "results-driven," since "the documents produced are more often briefs for the MBE program than an independent inquiry into the existence of discrimination."[13] Some studies have not met the conditions set forth in *Croson,* failing for one reason or another to make the proper comparison. Some have produced little more then "societal discrimination"—which the Court rejects. LaNoue points out that this massive effort to prove discrimination already has cost taxpayers $45 million. Some of the money has even come from the federal government.

The judicial outlook for disparity studies is not good. Some district courts have approved them, others have not, and rolled into any judgment about a study's legal validity is the technical question of whether it is okay to present evidence of discrimination *after* the program has been adopted. So far the only disparity study to be reviewed by a federal appeals court (for the city of Philadelphia) has received an emphatic rejection.

Nonetheless, because the validity of a study cannot be determined without a potentially lengthy trial that could involve expert testimony from economists and other social scientists, and because few private parties can incur the expense of this kind of litigation, even a flawed disparity study can serve to protect or prolong the use of race in contracting. Much turns on the depth of a government's commitment to using race, and there is no question that many governments are very deeply committed. In the wake of its loss in the California courts, the Los Angeles County Metropolitan Transportation Agency did not fold its set-aside hand but immediately commissioned disparity studies—to be carried out by minority-owned businesses who do business with it—in order to justify the agency's use of race. The next Michael Cornelius will have to weigh the cost of a trial in which his lawyers will be

forced to take on complex, if legally inadequate, studies purporting to demonstrate discrimination.

In *Croson,* the Supreme Court focused more on the predicate for a race-based remedy—evidence of discrimination—than on the remedy itself. But Justice O'Connor's comments about remedies have had some effect. Some jurisdictions with set-asides that were ridiculously overinclusive in terms of the groups targeted for the remedy have dropped the groups for which there is no evidence of discrimination; the best example is Richmond, whose revised set-aside program now targets only blacks—no Eskimos or Aleuts (or anyone else besides blacks) are given preference in the former capital of the Confederacy. O'Connor's condemnation of rigid numerical remedies has led some jurisdictions to make their use of race less obvious by resorting to "flexible goals" and by emphasizing that in meeting these goals race will be only "one factor" among many in a contracting decision. But no one should be under the illusion that such changes will end discrimination.

Consider a goal-oriented program from the state of California. The state's women and minority business enterprise law requires that electrical, gas, and telephone corporations draw up annual plans for increasing procurement on the part of women and minorities. The implementing order directs the utilities to buy "not less than 15 percent" of the products and services they need from minority-owned businesses (with minorities defined as blacks, Hispanics, Native Americans, and Asian-Pacific Americans) and "not less than 5 percent" from women-owned businesses. The order emphasizes that these are goals, however, "not quotas." It defines a goal as a "target which when achieved, indicates progress in a preferred direction." The order further says that a goal is not "a requirement." And under the order, a utility may not be sanctioned for failing to meet its goals, but only for failing to make acceptable progress toward them.

So far, it would seem, so good. But here's the catch: the sanction for insufficient progress could include a reduction in the utility's rate of return. So even though a goal may not explicitly require preferential treatment, a goal can strongly encourage it. Not surprisingly, in order to comply with the law, one California utility—Pacific Bell—developed a preferential scheme that uses race as "one factor" among many. Already we can see how this one factor can become the determining factor and thus discriminate against someone lacking the necessary race.

In 1991, Pacific Bell decided to "pre-qualify" architectural firms in the San Francisco Bay area. Those selected would enjoy what the utility called "improved business partnerships"—meaning it would contract with the firms for architectural services. Interested firms filled out a "pre-qualification criteria" form that included this question: "Are you currently certified through the Cordoba Corporation Clearing House process for Minority/Women Business Enterprise status?" J. Jack Bras, who is white, and who had been a contractor with Pacific Bell since 1969, completed this form, answering the certification question in the negative. In due course, Bras learned that thirteen firms in all had submitted forms, and that Pacific Bell, basing its decisions entirely on the information contained in those forms, had decided to do business with the firms that ranked one, two, and three. Bras also learned that he had made the sixth spot, but would have been ranked third had Pacific Bell not considered the answers to the certification question. As it happened, the utility awarded firms ten points for answering the question "yes," and zero points for the answer Bras gave. The third-

ranking firm was minority-owned. But for the one factor of
race, Bras would have secured an "improved business part-
nership" with Pacific Bell.[14]

Resistance in Washington

Incorporating the strict scrutiny analysis of *Croson,* the
Adarand decision imperils the federal government's use of
race in contracting and other programs. Like many state and
local governments in the wake of *Croson,* the Clinton administration is trying to come up with "findings" of discrimination that might serve as a compelling interest. It's obvious
why the administration assigned itself this job: it is committed to preferences, and yet few, if any, of the federal programs
containing preferences were originally justified in terms the
Court would now approve.

Sponsors of preferences in federal contracting typically
have pointed to "societal discrimination." No more specific
"evidence" has been available because the low-bid process
used in contracting leaves little room for discrimination.
Unlike voting, employment, and education, where there have
been many judicial findings of discrimination against
minorities, there appear to be no modern cases of discrimination by a government against a low-bidding minority business enterprise.[15]

The question is whether the administration can do a better job of "proving discrimination" in a way the Court might
accept. It's one thing to produce a disparity study for a locality, as researchers could search for evidence of discrimination in a specific market, but at the federal level, as George
LaNoue points out, there is the problem of deciding which

market should be examined, given that business conditions vary widely across the country.[16]

The administration's resistance to *Adarand* will preserve the status quo unless Congress intervenes by passing color-blind law. Of course, litigation based on *Adarand* could itself bring about the demise of preferences. Indeed, that process has already begun. In the fall of 1995, a lawsuit forced the administration to suspend a Defense Department program used in awarding contracts known as the Rule of Two. Under this program, contracts were automatically reserved for a minority-owned firm whenever two or more such businesses had submitted proper bids; only these firms would be allowed to compete. The clearly exclusionary nature of the program was in violation of the Court's interpretation of the Constitution. Facing a losing battle in the courts, the admin-istration scrapped the Rule of Two but did not quit its attach-ment to preferences. The Rule of Two happened to be only a means to an end — that of awarding at least 5 percent of Pen-tagon contract dollars to minority firms. In a press release, the Defense Department stated its intention to use other means of achieving that numerical goal.

One means available to the Pentagon and the rest of the government is the "bid preference" under which contracting officers may add up to 10 percent to the bids submitted by nonminority firms, thus making it possible for originally higher-bidding minority businesses to win the contract. Here, race is "one factor" among many — meaning, of course, that it is the decisive factor. A 1995 lawsuit challenging a bid prefer-ence shows how the bid-preference procedure works and the discrimination it inflicts. Kay & Associates, Inc., a nonminor-ity airplane maintenance firm, learned from the Navy that it had submitted the lowest bid, $38.5 million, for a contract to maintain aircraft. But the Navy then added 10 percent to the firm's bid in order to favor a minority firm, which had bid $39.1 million. Settling the lawsuit before trial, the administration retained the bid-preference procedure and even contemplated its extension to other departments and agencies.

The Wrong Answer

Preferential treatment in contracting is the wrong answer to reasonable questions—assuming these are questions its supporters care to ask. If the question is discrimination on the part of a contracting officer, the victim should have a process available for seeking redress. The same holds if the question is one of discrimination on the part of a prime contractor in the award of a subcontract. If the question is one of discrimination in lending or bonding, the law should furnish a process to enforce prohibitions against such practices. And if the question is one of making intelligible and accessible to all parties a government's contracting opportunities, surely that can be done without resorting to preferences.

But the history of preferences in contracting reveals little interest in these questions. Instead, governments have been far more interested simply in ensuring that certain constituents get "a fair share of the action." In 1985, for example, when Baltimore formally adopted its set-aside program, it did so without even making a bow toward any need to remedy past discrimination. The stated purposes of the ordinance concerned economic development on the part of minorities—that is, a fair share of the action.

Baltimore also serves to illustrate another possibility—that of a majority composed of minorities whose representatives legislate references in their behalf, thus discriminating against the nonminorities who constitute the minority of the jurisdiction's population. In the *Croson* case, Justice O'Connor showed that she was not naive. Taking note of Richmond's black-majority city council, she observed that the set-aside might well have been motivated by "simple racial politics."

The potential for racial politics of this kind in the nation's largest cities is substantial. In 1993, George LaNoue calculated that groups eligible for affirmative action constitute a majority of the total population in twelve of the nation's twenty largest cities, and that more than half of the twelve had mayors from minority groups during the previous decade.[17] Demographic trends suggest that the majority populations of our largest cities will continue to be made up of minorities eligible for affirmative action.

At the federal level, there has been no interest in ferreting out any discrimination in contracting, such as it might be. Here, too, the story has been one of ensuring "a fair share of the action." Consider, for example, the set-aside provision included in the Energy Policy Act of 1992. The provision required that at least 10 percent of all federal contracts for energy conservation in government buildings, purchase of natural-gas–powered vehicles, and energy research and development be awarded to small businesses owned by minorities or women. The set-aside was a late and quiet addition to the bill. According to the *Washington Post*, the provision "was hardly mentioned in all the months of hearings and floor debates over nuclear power, offshore oil drilling, and expanded use of natural gas"—the principal subjects of the legislation. Representative John Conyers of Michigan, who is not known for his interest in energy policy and, according to the *Post*, "kept quiet so as not to arouse opposition from legislators opposed to affirmative action 'quotas,' " managed to slip the provision into the bill at the last minute.[18] That Conyers was simply ensuring "a fair share of the action" for minorities and women is a reasonable inference. The set-aside did not require proof that its beneficiaries had suffered discrimination in government contracting or in their business affairs generally. Nor did Congress justify the set-aside with any finding that the legally preferred groups had endured past discrimination in federal contracting.

The oldest and largest federal set-aside program remains the one administered by the Small Business Administration. Its Minority Enterprise Development Program is supposed to help "economically disadvantaged" minorities, but participants in the program may be doing quite well, given that the conditions imposed upon participants allow a net worth of up to $250,000, excluding home and business equity, when a contract is first awarded, and up to $750,000 thereafter. As it happens, some of the "economically disadvantaged" are even better off than the program allows. A recent audit conducted by the SBA's inspector general found that 35 of 50 randomly selected participants had net worths of more than $1 million, and 12 of the 50 received annual compensation in excess of $750,000. A fair share of the action, indeed.

Racial Teachings

In his dissent in *Fullilove,* Justice Potter Stewart wrote, "By making race a relevant criterion . . . in its own affairs, government teaches the public that the apportionment of rewards and penalties can legitimately be made according to race . . . and that people can, and perhaps should, view themselves and others in terms of their racial characteristics."

The groups now officially preferred by the federal government in contracting programs are blacks, Hispanics, Native Americans, and Asian-Pacific Americans. The last group includes persons from Burma, Thailand, Malaysia, Indonesia, Singapore, Brunei, Japan, China, Taiwan, Laos, Cambodia, Vietnam, Korea, the Philippines, U.S. Trust Territory of the Pacific Islands, Republic of the Marshall Islands, Federated States of Micronesia, the Commonwealth of the Northern Mariana Islands, Guam, Samoa, Macao, Hong Kong, Fiji, Tonga, Kiribati, Tuvalu, Mauru, India, Pakistan, Bangladesh, Sri Lanka, Bhutan, the Maldives Islands, and Nepal.

As for the states, the pacesetter here has been California, whose Public Contract Code makes eligible for its contracting preferences a citizen or lawful permanent resident who is:

> an ethnic person of color and who is: Black (a person having origins in any of the Black racial groups of Africa); Hispanic (a person of Mexican, Puerto Rican, Cuban, Central or South American, or other Spanish or Portuguese culture or origin regardless of race); Native American (an American Indian, Eskimo, Aleut, or Native Hawaiian); Pacific-Asian (a person whose origins are from Japan, China, Taiwan, Korea, Vietnam, Laos, Cambodia, the Philippines, Samoa, Guam, or the United States Trust Territories of the Pacific including the Northern Marianas); Asian-Indian (a person whose origins are from India, Pakistan, or Bangladesh).

The Public Contract Code provides for the discretionary expansion of this list: "or any other group of natural persons identified as minorities in the respective project specifications of an awarding department or participating local agency."

Some people are not offended by the racial and ethnic distinctions government draws. They have no trouble with the idea that government should encourage thinking in racial terms, and they are confident that racial regulation can be done to good effect. They will not be easily dissuaded from their position. Yet we need only consider the history of our country to see that when government makes racial distinctions, bad things do follow.

In the *Adarand* case, Justice O'Connor gently rebuked the racial engineers when she wrote, "it may not always be clear that a so-called preference is in fact 'benign.'" Those bumped aside by preferences—a Thomas Stewart or a Jack Bras— know how "benign" they are. But preferences also can have negative effects for their ostensible beneficiaries.

On the eve of the *Adarand* decision, one minority entrepreneur who eschews set-asides told the *Wall Street Journal* that they suggest "minorities aren't bright enough, aren't competent enough, or don't work hard enough to compete with white businesses." Another commented that the stigma of winning contracts as a minority "cheapens everything I've accomplished." Another said that he purposely steered clear of racially coded grants because they instill "this feeling of entitlement."[19]

Justice Clarence Thomas understands these concerns. Indeed, in his concurring opinion in *Adarand*, Thomas discussed the non-benign character of preferences. "So-called benign discrimination," he wrote, "teaches many that because of chronic and apparently immutable handicaps, minorities cannot compete . . . without . . . patronizing indulgence. . . . These programs stamp minorities with a badge of inferiority and may cause them to develop dependencies or to adopt an attitude that they are 'entitled' to preferences."

Thomas's policy argument is careful and powerful. The justice said that preferences teach "many" people, not everyone, that minorities can't make it. And he did not say that preferences invariably cause "dependencies" or feelings of "entitlement" on the part of its ostensible beneficiaries, only that they *may* do that. Thomas's argument thus is not blind to the cases in which "affirmative action babies" have grown up to do quite well, who do not depend on preferences nor think they must be given them. In sum, his argument is not that preferences always produce bad consequences for their beneficiaries, only that they often do. And because we cannot know in advance what the results of preferential treatment in any particular case will be, we are better off forgoing it altogether.

The New Republic's Jeff Rosen summarized Thomas's argument this way: "Perhaps not all affirmative action is stigmatizing; but anything short of an absolute ban would not adequately distinguish between racial classifications that produce stigma and those that don't. Because so much is stigmatizing, all must be banned."[20]

7

The Immigration Factor

Tim Jennings is the owner of an industrial equipment firm in Long Island City, New York. In late 1993, he submitted the lowest bid on two New York City jobs, but did not win either one. Instead, under a policy requiring that 20 percent of the city's business go to minority and women-owned business enterprises, the city gave the jobs to a firm in Lodi, New Jersey. This company was owned by an Asian-Indian named Vijay Patel. When Jennings complained about the decision, officials told him that the city was trying "to redress discrimination that such companies experienced prior to the implementation of this program." But Patel, a recent immigrant, told the *New York Post* that he had never experienced discrimination in his business.[1]

Jennings was understandably upset, having lost business on account of his race. But when we look from another angle at the affirmative action program that Jennings encountered, two additional points are evident. First, the program prefers immigrants over native-born citizens. Second, the program extends a benefit to some immigrants that is not available to others. Had Jennings been a Russian immigrant, he would have been no better off in the "competition" with Vijay Patel.

In opening its affirmative action arms to certain immigrants, the New York City set-aside program is not unusual. Most legal immigrants who possess the necessary race or ethnicity are in theory eligible for most affirmative action programs. (Immigration law prohibits the hiring of illegal immigrants.) Private employers may hire and promote immigrants to reach the racial and ethnic totals necessary to avoid disparate impact liability under Title VII. Those who contract with the federal government and are therefore regulated by the Office of Federal Contracts Compliance Programs (OFCCP) are not barred from employing immigrants to meet their numerical goals. In the public sector, while the federal government makes U.S. citizenship a condition of employment, most states and localities do not. The U.S. Small Business Administration's set-aside program also requires participants to be U.S. citizens—which means, of course, that a recently arrived immigrant who has become a citizen may participate. As for state and local governments, many of them do not require citizenship for participation in their set-aside programs. Most other programs involving preferences, regardless of the level of government, do not exclude legal immigrants.

As we saw in chapter 3, affirmative action was originally justified in terms of remedying past discrimination and its lingering ill effects. The remedial rationale held that some Americans had discriminated against other Americans (or persons who were in America); presumably, affirmative action would target individuals already living in the United States. What the founders of affirmative action did not foresee was that this rationale could not sustain what affirmative action would become, thanks to immigration. For that matter, the founders of affirmative action failed to think more broadly about the impact of immigration upon affirmative action (or of affirmative action upon immigration). Had eligibility for affirmative action been explicitly denied to future immigrants, immigration would not have created conceptual and practical difficulties for affirmative action.

Affirmative Action for Immigrants?

At the conceptual level, the remedial rationale, as articulated in the late 1960s, cannot sustain preferential treatment for a population produced by immigration since, say, 1970. Whatever past wrongs might have been committed against this population were committed elsewhere, in other countries by other people. The members of this population are "owed" nothing by Americans. This point holds equally for someone who immigrated here from sub-Saharan Africa in 1980 and for a 1980 immigrant from Barcelona or Mexico City or Seoul or Hong Kong.

Is there any way to justify affirmative action for recent immigrants? As we saw in previous chapters, the other rationales typically offered for affirmative action—proportionalism and diversity—are flawed. Proportionalism and diversity can no more sustain affirmative action for immigrants than they can for anyone else. In recent years, advocates of affirmative action have offered, in effect, yet another rationale—that preferences are necessary to prevent future discrimination that awaits people of color, including those freshly arrived in the United States. The message this rationale sends to immigrants is indeed curious. "Americans," writes Lawrence H. Fuchs, vice-chair of the United States Commission on Immigration Reform and author of *The American Kaleidoscope: Race, Ethnicity, and the Civic Culture,* "have gone further than any other multiethnic nation in developing a human and decent multiethnic society."[2] Yet for some reason we tell more than a million people who annually come to our shores that they will be discriminated against and need preferences to get ahead.

Fuchs himself has concluded that there is no "plausible reason why immigrants (and their children) who have come to America voluntarily in the last two decades should qualify for affirmative action." Fuchs says that affirmative action for immigrants "is bad for them and bad for the United States."[3] He explains that affirmative action is bad for immigrants because it sends the message that "they are entitled to special benefits merely because of their membership in a designated group"—a message "contrary to the American civil rights compact . . . of individual and not group rights." Fuchs makes this point carefully, as he should: he says that affirmative action sends a message, not that immigrants invariably agree with and act upon it. Most immigrants come here without any knowledge of affirmative action. Still, the message is there, and there is some evidence it is being absorbed.

In 1994, the University of Maryland's George LaNoue, using documents gained through a freedom of information request, published a study of the Small Business Administration's decisions regarding eligibility for participation in affirmative action programs. In 1978, Congress authorized the SBA to set aside federal contracts for businesses owned by blacks, Hispanics, and Native Americans, while also giving the agency discretion to add other "socially or economically disadvantaged"

groups to the program. As LaNoue shows, the groups peti-
tioning for inclusion since 1978 have been those increased by
recent immigration. In 1979, Asian-Americans successfully
lobbied the SBA for recognition, followed in later years by
Asian-Indians (1982), Sri Lankans (1988), Tongans (1989), and
Indonesians (1989). The petitions by these groups emphasized
group discrimination, even when there was none, as in the
case of Tongans and Sri Lankans, recent newcomers to the
United States. Asian-Indians and Indonesians also emphasized group discrimination, even though the educational and
economic attainments of both groups are well above the
United States average. LaNoue found that the SBA decisions
to grant eligibility to these groups and to reject others (including Iranians) were best explained in terms of an "ideology of
color" argument—that skin color is an impediment to social
and economic advancement in America. If victimhood is what
the government rewards, it is not surprising that groups seeking to be included in affirmative action programs have peti-
tioned the way they have.[4]

Fuchs's other point—that affirmative action for immigrants is bad for the United States—is borne out by stories
like the one from New York City involving Tim Jennings and
Vijay Patel. Fuchs makes the case that affirmative action for
immigrants will create understandable resentment and division. Such programs pit native-born Americans against preferred immigrants and give preferred immigrants a leg up
over nonpreferred immigrants. Ironically, they also put preferred immigrants in competition with those living in the
United States whom affirmative action originally targeted.

An example comes from Ohio. In chapter 1 we met Jerry
Henry, a painter who in the 1980s was excluded on account
of his race (he is white) from bidding on certain construction
projects at Ohio State University. Henry ran into the state's

set-aside law, passed in 1980, which targeted blacks, Hispanics, American Indians, and Orientals. In 1991, the Republican Governor George Voinovich decided to include Asian-Indians —most of whom in Ohio are recent immigrants—within the Oriental category. Over the next two years, 64 Asian-Indian firms became certified and won contracts totaling $5.6 million. Black contractors who had won contracts over the years under the set-aside law were upset with the new affirmative action competition. One black contractor sued, seeking the exclusion of Asian-Indians from the Oriental category. The Asian-Indian contractors countersued. The dispute has a political dimension: in Ohio, Asian-Indians, who contributed $278,000 to Voinovich's 1990 campaign, tend to be Republicans, and most blacks are Democrats. In 1993, the state attorney general, a Democrat, said that the Republican governor had exceeded his authority by making Asian-Indians eligible for affirmative action and ordered the decertification of all 64 Asian-Indian firms. In 1994, a state judge who is a Republican overturned the attorney general's decision, predictably holding that "the common meaning of the term 'Oriental' includes Asian Indians."[5]

Such "affirmative-action-induced conflict," as Fuchs calls it, is also bad for America because it invites anti-immigrant sentiment, hardly an ennobling quality in a nation made up almost entirely of immigrants and the descendants of immigrants.

To be sure, immigrants are entitled to the equal protection of the laws. But they should not be eligible for affirmative action. Fuchs argues that the failure of the architects of affirmative action to limit eligibility to those in the United States prior to the early 1970s should now be addressed. Fuchs's recommendation has been met largely by silence from the political supporters of affirmative action.

The New Waves of Immigration

Immigration would not bear on the future of affirmative action without the substantial waves of immigration occurring since the late 1960s, coincidentally the beginning of affirmative action. To repeat, affirmative action for these immigrants is bad for them and bad for the country. But the immigration of recent years also has been having a profound impact upon the nation's demographics and therefore upon the groups targeted for affirmative action.

The surge of legal immigration over the past three decades was made possible by a change in federal law whose results no one predicted. In 1965, Congress amended the Immigration and Nationality Act, eliminating the bias of the old system in favor of Europeans. Sponsors of the amendments were confident that the level of immigration would stay the same, but with the old barriers lifted, the level increased, accompanied by a dramatic change in the nature of the immigrant population, as Asians and Hispanics poured into the country in huge numbers. These groups, as we know, also happened to have been designated for preferential treatment in America. Looking back, Peter Skerry has rightly observed that it was "an historical accident that the groups that received distinctive protection under civil-rights legislation and judicial rulings were shortly to expand greatly through immigration."[6]

According to census data, in 1970 Hispanics numbered 9 million, a figure that had climbed above 22 million by 1990, an increase of roughly 150 percent. In 1970, Asians numbered close to 1.5 million. In 1990, the census counted more than 7.2 million Asians—an almost fivefold increase. Meanwhile, the black population grew more slowly, from 22.5 million to almost 30 million, and the white population even less dramatically, from 180 million to almost 200 million, with most of the increase due to births, not immigration. The immigration trends continue to this day. In 1995, the Census Bureau said that 4.5 million people had immigrated during the first four years of the decade, the principal newcomers continuing to be Hispanics and Asians.

These facts, and their implications, are arresting. George LaNoue has calculated that during the 1970s the population of those eligible for affirmative action grew seven times faster than the population of those who are not so eligible, and more than five times faster during the 1980s.[7] The main explanation for this dynamic, of course, is the immigration of Hispanics and Asians. That immigration also has altered the character of the population eligible for affirmative action. In 1970, LaNoue shows, blacks comprised 66 percent of that population. By 1980, the proportion had declined to 57 percent, and by 1990 to 49 percent. The proportion of this population that is Hispanic and Asian, meanwhile, has increased. In 1970, it was 31 percent, in 1980 it had climbed to 38 percent, and in 1990, it was up to 48 percent. Today, there is no doubt that the Hispanic and Asian proportion is well above 50 percent of the affirmative-action population, and that it will only climb higher, because the demographic trends show no signs of changing. The upshot is that a policy begun to remedy historic discrimination against blacks is now a policy for which Hispanics and Asians stand to be the principal beneficiaries.

These facts raise the question whether Hispanics and Asians should continue to be included in affirmative action programs. While most institutions of higher education have dropped Asians from their preferential admissions roster on account of academic excellence, both Asians and Hispanics remain in most general programs, such as the one the U.S. Labor Department administers and those found in federal and state procurement. But, as Harvard University's Nathan Glazer reports, more than 50 percent of both the Hispanic and Asian populations in the United States now consist of immigrants and the children they have borne, meaning that affirmative action has become a policy that mainly targets groups mostly consisting of immigrants and their children. Whether affirmative action for Hispanics and Asians ever made sense, it no longer does.

For Blacks Only?

Recognizing the thirty-year impact of immigration upon affirmative action, Glazer and Fuchs, among others, have contended in recent years that preferential treatment should no longer be extended to Hispanics and Asians. For them, however, blacks are another case. Central to their argument for retaining preferences for blacks only is that no other group has a comparable history of oppression and that blacks, after all, were the original affirmative action group. Conceding that preferences are at odds with core American principles, Glazer and Fuchs contend that these principles should not stand in the way of affirmative action for blacks, at least not for another decade or two.[8]

This position invites those of us who argue against preferential treatment for any group to address the concerns of those who fear the impact upon blacks of ending affirmative action. Four concerns are typically voiced—concerns about racism, progress, segregation, and rejection. None of them, however, suffices as a reason to pull back from ending affirmative action.

- *Racism on the part of whites against blacks is widespread, entrenched in many institutions, and affirmative action is a necessary means of overcoming it.* Researchers agree that over the past half-century the views that whites have of blacks have changed dramatically for the better.[9] Among other things, the overwhelming majority of whites today say that they would vote for a black political candidate, and almost 100 percent of whites say that blacks and whites should have an equal chance to compete for jobs. As for the rising generation of whites, surveys of racial attitudes indicate that younger whites are at least as committed to equal rights for blacks as their elders.[10] Today, the discrimination that blacks experience is not the wall-to-wall variety of the Jim Crow era but episodic, in a particular context, and authorities usually move rapidly to enforce the multitude of laws that have been enacted to make plain our abhorrence as a society toward racial discrimination. In 1994, for example, the Denny's chain was quickly brought to justice when the news broke that some of its restaurants were discriminating against blacks; Denny's had to pay more than $54 million to settle the case. Nonetheless, those who cite racism as a reason not to end affirmative action for blacks contend that the phenomenon is so deeply embedded in our society that surveys of racial attitudes on the part of whites cannot be trusted, and that such periodic occurrences as the brutality committed by Los Angeles police against Rodney King and the 1995 murder of civilian blacks by white GIs in North Carolina—a racial-hate crime if ever there was one—reveal how whites really do see blacks. In this view, preferences are needed to counteract the pervasive racism that is constantly pushing blacks down.[11]

For obvious reasons, chief among them the inscrutability of the human heart, the question of how much racism truly exists in America is unanswerable. We do not ordinarily make policy, and should not in this case, on the basis of what can't be known. Besides, those who say we need preferences because of pervasive white racism typically make their case by citing statistics and anecdotes that fall far short of what the Supreme Court requires before a government may even think about resorting to preferences — "a solid basis in evidence" of discrimination.

No one should be discriminated against on account of race. That, thankfully, is a settled matter, a part of our national creed. But the best we can humanly do as a society is not to presume institutions guilty of racism or racial discrimination, and then resort to preferences that breed resentment and division, but to remain focused on actual instances of discriminatory behavior and demand vigorous law enforcement action against it. If more resources are necessary to ensure effective enforcement of the antidiscrimination laws, then our legislative bodies should provide them.

• *Without affirmative action, the material progress blacks have enjoyed would be slowed and perhaps even reversed.* Blacks made substantial progress *before* the institution of affirmative action programs (and even before the enactment of critical antidiscrimination measures).[12] As late as 1940, for example, the poverty rate for black families was 87 percent. But in the 1940s, blacks began acquiring the skills and education that led to better jobs, and by 1970 the poverty rate had declined to just above 30 percent. Also during this period, the number of blacks holding professional or technical jobs quadrupled. The question thus arises whether the best way to promote economic advancement among blacks is affirmative action. Given the negative effects of preferences, both for some recipients and for all of those bumped out of an opportunity on account of their "wrong" race, it is not obvious that preferences constitute the better path. Moreover, the fact that many blacks have advanced without affirmative action is compelling evidence of their ability to achieve. Precisely because preferences have created doubt about the abilities and achievements of blacks, both among blacks and the public at large, ending the policy would remove the basis for those doubts.

Concern about a braking or halting of material progress touches on the important matter of the black middle class. Years ago it was argued that a much larger black middle class was in the nation's best interest and that the jump start of affirmative action might help produce that. But this argument recognized that such a jump start should be temporary and that the suspension of colorblind principle it required must not become permanent. Today, of course, there is indeed a large black middle class. If, for the sake of argument, we credit preferences in large part for this development, we still must ask whether affirmative action really should be maintained for the sons and daughters of middle- and upper-class black couples. Black economic progress actually should make ending affirmative action an easier task: the very existence of this middle class creates its own momentum for further progress, since family income correlates with the educational achievement of children and thus their social and economic advancement.

- *Blacks and whites live in separate worlds, and affirmative action is necessary to integrate the nation.* To the extent that this concern is about the so-called underclass of blacks, which numbers between 2 and 3 million of the total black population of 31 million, and in which the problems of illegal drugs, criminal violence, educational failure, family instability, and homelessness are severe, it must be said that affirmative action can do very little to improve such conditions. Those whom the sociologist William Julius Wilson calls the "truly disadvantaged" lack the threshold skills needed even to be considered for an opportunity under an affirmative action program.[13] Nonetheless, some advocates of affirmative action continue to point to the underclass as though it were an argument for policies aimed at those positioned *above* the underclass. It can be no such thing. The conditions of the underclass constitute an American tragedy that merits the attention of public officials and private-sector leaders alike. But the underclass cannot logically be cited in an effort to maintain programs designed to benefit, as Wilson puts it, "minority individuals from the most advantaged families."

The concern about separation and integration, then, must be clarified, in this way: *Without affirmative action, blacks in position to benefit from it would not advance as far as they would otherwise, with less integration the unfortunate result.* Defending affirmative action, Nicholas Lemann contemplates in its absence nothing less than "an enormous decrease in black representation everywhere in white-collar (and also blue-collar) America."[14] But the more likely result would be decreases in integration in some places and increases in others, but overall little net change. For example, studies show that the OFCCP's enforcement of numerical affirmative action has redistributed black workers from nonregulated to regulated firms.[15] If the OFCCP's effort were ended tomorrow, there could be a reshuffling of jobs held by blacks, with some firms becoming more integrated than others. Not only would the overall level of integration remain roughly the same, but there would be no question about how jobs were obtained, preferences having been removed as an explanation. In higher education, if affirmative action were ended today, there would be many fewer blacks enrolling in the nation's most elite schools tomorrow. This prospect is what especially worries Glazer and other defenders of preferences for blacks. But blacks for many years now have been able to gain admission to Harvard, for example, on the same academic terms as those admitted under regular standards, and as blacks continue to register educational gains, more blacks probably will be able to compete for admission to Harvard on the same basis as all other students. Meanwhile, blacks who would have been enrolled at Harvard under affirmative action would still be going to classes at some of the nation's better schools. Which is to say: if there is less integration at Harvard, there will be more integration somewhere else, and, again, the integration will be on terms that do not cast doubt upon the abilities and achievements of blacks.

- *Blacks will regard ending affirmative action as a terrible rejection by an indifferent and hostile society.* It is indeed possible to do the right thing for the wrong reason, and if it became apparent that the central motivation for ending affirmative action were to do harm to blacks, that would be a sufficient reason to have serious second thoughts. But is opposition to affirmative action mainly a product of bad motive? Some supporters of affirmative action say it is and that most opponents are really racists. The best evidence says otherwise. In their 1993 study *The Scar of Race*, the political scientists Paul M. Sniderman of Stanford University and Thomas Piazza of the University of California at Berkeley concluded that, while prejudice has not disappeared, it "no longer organizes and dominates the reactions of whites; it no longer leads large numbers of them to oppose public policies to assist blacks across-the-board." Their data show that white racism is not "the primary factor driving the contemporary arguments over the politics of race." Instead, whites oppose affirmative action mainly because it violates "convictions about fairness and fair play that make up the American Creed." Sniderman and Piazza put the point precisely: "The principle of preferential treatment runs against the Creed. . . . It produces resentment and disaffection not because it assists blacks . . . but because it is judged to be unfair."[16] The authors also found that many whites who oppose affirmative action are willing to support other programs that benefit blacks. (Presumably, these would be race-neutral programs that disproportionately assist blacks, such as increasing resources for inner-city schools or offering tax breaks and other economic incentives to businesses willing to relocate in inner-city neighborhoods. Such ideas have drawn support from conservatives as well as liberals, Republicans as well as Democrats.) Two subsequent studies in which Sniderman also was involved lend further support to the conclusions of *The Scar of Race*.[17]

Despite the results of these studies, traditional civil rights leaders continue to impute racism to those opposed to affirmative action. It is possible that they may succeed in convincing a majority of blacks to view ending affirmative action as a cruel rejection by the majority white society. Ultimately, therefore, the real issue is that of responsible leadership. We should bear in mind that opinion surveys have consistently shown substantial numbers of

blacks, sometimes majorities, to be opposed to preferences.[18] The concern for fair treatment of individuals independent of race knows no racial boundaries.

The Immigrant Nation and Colorblind Law

The question that the American experiment ultimately raises
is whether we have any choice but colorblind law. From the
start we have been an immigrant nation, and our creed
endorses the proposition that anyone can become an American, regardless of race or country of origin. Yet we do not
have to be reminded that race and ethnicity have proved to
be deeply divisive in our culture. And from our own experience we have learned that law which distinguishes and discriminates on the basis of race has only reinforced division
and badly damaged the nation.

In contrast, colorblind law provides equal protection for
individuals in every racial or ethnic group by denying to any
group a position of favoritism or subordination. As applied to
government, colorblind law denies to any racial and ethnic
group that controls the levers of power that it may use that
power to benefit its own constituents at the expense of others. It relieves government of the extraordinary difficulty of
determining just who should be favored and who should not
be, a task made more problematic today by the growing numbers of mixed-race marriages. Ultimately, colorblind law
forces the search for political consensus into nonracial territory. In a nation in which economic and political power is
now being more widely shared among people of different
races and ethnic groups—a trend likely to continue—colorblind law makes eminently practical sense.

8

The Ground Shifts

As we have seen, affirmative action was hatched during the 1960s and 1970s in federal bureaucracies and in the councils of leadership of higher education. Soon thereafter, it won the approval of the Supreme Court. Though it had the support of both Republicans and Democrats in its formative years, by the late 1970s the two parties had begun to divide on the issue. While the Democratic Party became more and more firmly attached to preferences, the GOP under Ronald Reagan grew more skeptical, though his administration failed to take action within its authority to eliminate preferences from federal programs. In the early 1990s, the battle between the Democratic Congress and the Bush administration over legislation concerning affirmative action in employment hardened the parties' positions.

By then, too, a large gap on the issue had opened between the elites who run the Democratic Party and its traditional working-class constituency. The former were as dedicated to preferential affirmative action policies as the latter were opposed, and working-class Democrats — the so-called "Reagan Democrats" — had been voting more and more often with the Republican Party. Moderates within the Democratic Party, concerned about the party's viability in presidential elections and its future generally, called for reconsideration of its strong support for preferences. In 1991, the Democratic Leadership Council (DLC), the nesting place of those who styled themselves New Democrats, issued a statement declaring opposition to "quotas that create racial, gender, or ethnic preferences." The DLC recognized that so long as old-style Democrats controlled Congress, there was little chance that the party's position would significantly change, but the New Democrats held out hope that their party's position could be altered through the forceful executive leadership of a moderate Democratic president.

In his 1992 campaign, Bill Clinton called himself "a new kind of Democrat," but upon taking office, it became clear that he would not become a DLC–style affirmative action reformer. With issues other than affirmative action preoccupying the high councils of the Clinton administration, policy in this area was largely left to appointees in the agencies with enforcement responsibilities — liberal Democrats dedicated to the defense and expansion of racial preferences. As one senior White House official says, "We gave civil rights over to the 'groups.' We looked at it as a reward to those who had been out of power for so long."

Clinton turned repeatedly to people from the "groups" in making appointments to key positions in the Justice, Education, and Labor departments. Lani Guinier, Clinton's nomi-

nee to be assistant attorney general for civil rights, was a former litigator for the NAACP Legal Defense and Educational
Fund; she expressed a view typical of those in her ideological circles when she said, in a law review article, that the term
"antidiscrimination" incorporates "a result-oriented inquiry,
in which roughly equal outcomes, not merely an apparently
fair process, are the goal." When Guinier proved too controversial a choice—for reasons related to her views on voting
rights—Clinton turned to Deval Patrick, another Legal
Defense Fund veteran. Indeed, virtually every key affirmative
action enforcement position was filled by a person who once
had worked for one of the liberal, pro–affirmative action
activist groups. Gilbert Casellas, chairman of the EEOC, had
served as national chairman of the Hispanic National Bar
Association as well as on the staff of the Puerto Rican Legal
Defense and Educational Fund. EEOC commissioner Paul
Igasaki had been executive director of the Asian Law Caucus.
Shirley Wilcher, the head of the Labor Department's Office
of Federal Contract Compliance Programs, had worked for
the National Women's Law Center. Norma Cantu, assistant
secretary of education for the office of civil rights, had been
a lawyer for the Mexican-American Legal Defense and Educational Fund. Other persons of similar backgrounds were
named to staff positions below the assistant secretary level.
Patrick's deputies included Kerry Scanlon of the NAACP
Legal Defense and Educational Fund and Isabelle Pinzler of
the ACLU's Women's Rights Project.

   In pursuing the defense and expansion of affirmative
action, these officials acted in the evident belief that the
Democratic control of both ends of Pennsylvania Avenue
implied broad national support for their agenda, even though
there was overwhelming evidence to the contrary provided by
opinion surveys. For example, Deval Patrick publicly accused

the Reagan and Bush administrations of "twelve years of sometimes neglect and sometimes active hostility to civil rights progress" and called a 1993 Supreme Court voting rights decision "alternately naive and venal." Remarks like these made the few New Democrats in the administration wince, but in the summer of 1994 the Clinton administration left no doubt about the direction of its affirmative action policy when the Justice Department, in a decision made by Patrick, announced its intention to switch sides in the case involving the Piscataway High School teacher Sharon Taxman, thereby supporting the board's decision to discharge her as lawful affirmative action justified in the name of "diversity."

While some administration officials (including Walter Dellinger, the head of the Justice Department's Office of Legal Counsel) privately expressed disagreement with Patrick's decision, the president refused to overrule him. At a White House press conference, President Clinton stated that he supported Patrick's decision and explained how it would be okay by him if, assuming racially opposite facts, the board had decided for the sake of diversity to "keep the white teacher." According to one White House aide, the president had no choice but to stick with Patrick, for if he had overruled him, he then would have had to answer to "the groups," with the worst-case scenario being a primary challenge from Jesse Jackson in 1996. Ironically, Clinton's 1993 decision to drop the Guinier nomination may have bonded him even more tightly to the groups. "Because we didn't stick with her," says the aide, "we had to be extra good."

It strains credulity, however, to regard Bill Clinton as an unwilling or unwitting participant in this drama, for Patrick's decision in the *Piscataway* case was entirely consistent with the broad affirmative action themes Clinton had sounded from the moment he took office. After all, as he himself often said, "diversity" was one criterion he used in staffing an administration that "looks like America" in terms of race, ethnicity, and sex. Moreover, prior to the reversal in the Piscataway case, his administration had aggressively pursued affirmative action—by reversing a Bush policy limiting the use of minority-exclusive scholarships, by defending hiring and promotion quotas in Birmingham and Memphis. Even Hillary Rodham Clinton's task force on health care reform pushed for diversity, calling for a health-care workforce that would achieve "sufficient racial, ethnic, gender, geographic, and cultural diversity to be representative of the people it services."

Though the switch in the *Piscataway* case left no doubt about the direction of Clinton's policy, affirmative action was not a major political issue in Washington during the first two years of his term. Congressional Republicans, still the minority party, were not in a position to confront the administration over its affirmative action policies, nor were they able to oppose expansions of affirmative action proposed by the Democrats in control of Capitol Hill. In fact, in the weeks just before the 1994 election, they went along with a provision buried in a larger bill that extended to the rest of the government a Defense Department affirmative action procedure for contracting. The measure authorized all departments and agencies to use "bid preferences" in which a minority may bid as high as 10 percent above the nonminority low bidder and still win the contract. Congress's extension of the bid-preference policy was so uncontroversial—it passed almost unanimously—that the press might well have interpreted it as a triumph of bipartisanship in behalf of affirmative action.

But then, suddenly, the GOP triumph in the 1994 midterm elections transformed the political landscape. Where congressional Democrats had for the most part been able to frame the terms of debate over domestic policy, now congressional Republicans could do so, and they could work their will on a full range of issues of their choosing, including affirmative action. It did not matter that the House Republicans' "Contract with America" had not mentioned affirmative action, nor that it had not been an explicit issue in any House or Senate race. The dramatic changing of the guard made possible a new congressional view of a whole raft of issues, affirmative action among them.

There had long been a possibility that affirmative action might finally be put in the political dock, simply because polls have consistently revealed large majorities opposed to preferences. In 1978, political scientists Seymour Martin Lipset and William Schneider reviewed public opinion on affirmative action and concluded that "every major national study shows that a sizable majority of Americans are opposed to remedying the effects of past discrimination by giving any special consideration in hiring or school admissions."[1] In 1992, Lipset reported similar findings, based on Gallup poll data from the period 1977–89. Gallup asked the following question: "Some people say that to make up for past discrimination, women and minorities should be given preferential treatment in getting jobs and places in college. Others say that ability, as determined by test scores, should be the main consideration. Which point of view comes close to how you feel on the subject?" Lipset pointed out that in each survey, 81 to 84 percent replied "ability" and 10 to 11 percent said "preferential treatment." In 1989, 56 percent of blacks responding to this question favored "ability" while 14 percent backed preferential treatment, as opposed to seven percent of whites. Between 1987 and 1990, Gallup changed the wording, as follows: "We should make every effort to improve the position of blacks and other minorities even if it means giving them preferential treatment." Here, majorities slightly in excess of 70 percent opposed preferential treatment, with 24 percent supporting it. Two-thirds of blacks surveyed for these polls rejected preferences, with 32 percent supporting them, compared to 18 percent of whites. And more than 80 percent of Republicans and two-thirds of Democrats responding to the question opposed preferences.[2] Reviewing survey data from 1985 to 1994, Everett Carll Ladd wrote in 1995 that blacks "see a greater need for affirmative action on their behalf than do their white fellow citizens," but he also observed that "on a great many aspects" of affirmative action "the story is not one of group differences but of agreement across racial ... lines." Ladd found that over the ten years in question the public had grown even less inclined "to see a need for temporary efforts in such areas as hiring and promotion that grant preference to make up for past denials of opportunity."[3]

No one can say for sure what accounts for this weakening degree of support. Several explanations come to mind: the failure of a temporary policy to be temporary; the accumulating force of its discriminatory and racially balkanizing tendencies; its implications concerning the abilities and achievements of those it targets; its paternalistic flavor; its association with intrusive government, increasingly unpopular; the patent unfairness of affirmative action for immigrants; generational change in which young people with no memory of Selma are unmoved by appeals referring to it; perhaps even the resistance of states and localities to the Court's decision in the *Croson* case. What is clear is that ending affirmative action was not politically plausible until the voters made their decision in 1994 to put Republicans in charge of Congress.

The new political circumstances ushered in by the election led in the first half of 1995 to the most focused, enduring consideration of the policy that we have ever had, with some programs containing preferences actually being eliminated. Thanks to the Supreme Court's June 1995 decision in the *Adarand* case, the political scrutiny being applied to affirmative action preferences only intensified. From Washington to the states, new laws were proposed that would to one degree or another end preferential affirmative action. Even President Clinton, shell-shocked by the midterm election, understood that the ground had shifted. "Affirmative action should not go on forever," he declared.

The boldest of the proposals represented efforts to recover colorblind law. They drew upon an insight that arose with increasing frequency during the affirmative action era: that law guaranteeing nondiscrimination for everyone, regardless of race, must in no uncertain terms outlaw preferential treatment. That is, law seeking to guarantee nondiscrimination must specify that race may not be a source of disadvantage *or* advantage for *any* person.

The California Dream

The earthquake in American politics was felt most powerfully in California. In October 1995, sponsors of the California Civil Rights Initiative (CCRI) began collecting the signatures needed — almost 700,000 — in order to have the measure placed on the November 1996 ballot. An effort to recover the original intent of the Civil Rights Act of 1964, after which it is named, the initiative would amend the state constitution in these terms: "The state shall not discriminate against, or grant preferential treatment to, any individual or group on the basis of race, sex, color, ethnicity, or national origin in the operation of public employment, public education, or public contracting." CCRI thus takes aim at all forms of discrimination, including that which results from preferential treatment. It would not outlaw nondiscriminatory affirmative action programs, such as those used in recruitment and training. By prohibiting discrimination based on sex as well as race, CCRI recognizes that there is no separate case to be made for preferential treatment based on gender. In California as elsewhere, affirmative action for women shares many of the same rationales as affirmative action for blacks and other minorities, and employs the same preferential techniques—"goals and timetables," "bid preferences," and so on.

Long the state most symbolic of New World opportunity, California during the affirmative action era has continued to grow in terms of both population and racial and ethnic diversity as state officials have pursued perhaps the most aggressive preference policies found anywhere in the country. The population climbed from 19 million in 1970 to 31 million in 1995, exceeding Canada's. Californians can trace their roots back to 150 different countries. Non-Hispanic whites constitute 57 percent of the population, Latinos 26 percent, Asians and Pacific Islanders 9 percent, and blacks 7 percent. Twenty-five percent of the population—the largest proportion of any state in the nation—is foreign-born. California promises to become more racially and ethnically jumbled in the years to come, not only as a result of immigration but also because of intermarriage, since a third to a half of Latinos and Asians in California now marry outside their ethnic group. Those eligible for most of the state's many affirmative action programs encompass all but the non-Hispanic white males, leaving 73 percent of all Californians who may be said to have a self-interest, narrowly understood, in maintaining affirmative action. But polls surveying opinion in the state have consistently found two-thirds favoring CCRI, with no difference between men and women, and with 40 to 50 percent of blacks and Latinos backing the measure.

The state code alone suggests the far-ranging nature of California's pursuit of affirmative action. For example, all state departments and agencies must establish in their personnel policies "goals and timetables designed to overcome any identified underutilization of minorities and women in their respective organizations." "Underutilization" is defined as merely having "fewer persons of a particular group in an occupation or at a level in a department that would reasonably be expected by their availability"—a definition similar to that found in the federal government's regulations implementing Executive Order 11246, which imposes numerical affirmative action upon federal contractors.

Another example: the governing board of each community college district must establish goals and timetables for hiring and promoting for administrative, faculty, and other positions "persons who are underrepresented in the work force compared to their number in the population, including . . . women and persons of racial and ethnic backgrounds." Pursuit of a goal can entail passing over qualified candidates in favor of less qualified persons "who may become qualified through appropriate training or experience within a reasonable length of time." Districts achieving their goals receive payments from a state "diversity fund." The money is a reimbursement for the administrative costs of affirmative action but also a bonus of sorts that may be pocketed. Thus it pays to discriminate.

State law also ensures preferences in procurement. The state treasurer must award at least 15 percent of the annual value of professional services contracts involved in the sale of

California bonds to minority-owned firms and at least 5 percent to those owned by women. The law defines "minority" as "an ethnic person of color including American Indians, Asians (including, but not limited to, Chinese, Japanese, Koreans, Pacific Islanders, Samoans, and Southeast Asians), Blacks, Filipinos, and Hispanics." The director of the California lottery also has a set-aside duty: the director must demand of those bidding for contracts (on jobs related to the administration of the lottery) that they subcontract a portion of the work to "socially and economically disadvantaged" enterprises, defined as minorities and women. Like most set-asides, this one was adopted in order to secure "the advancement of business opportunities" for those it makes eligible — in theory the overwhelming majority of the state's population. And then there is the set-aside labor of the general services department, which is forbidden by law from awarding contracts for commodities, services, and construction to the lowest bidder, unless that bidder promises to subcontract work to minorities and women.

The California Civil Rights Initiative is the creation of two professors new to grassroots political activism — Tom Wood, executive director of the California Association of Scholars and a former philosophy professor, and Glynn Custred, a professor of anthropology at California State University, Hayward. "Since we both worked in higher education," says Wood, "we had seen how aggressive and how pernicious affirmative action in California had become." In 1991, they saw how much more aggressive and more pernicious it might become when the Democratically controlled legislature passed a bill that, but for a veto by Governor Pete Wilson, would have pressured the university system to use preferences to achieve racial and ethnic proportionalism in admissions and even graduation.

Assembly Bill No. 2150 was a bold proposal indeed. In the euphemistic clothing of "educational equity," the bill represented affirmative action in its fullest, most grotesque evolution into a policy whose dedication to a mindless proportionalism would have undermined academic merit while guaranteeing racial and ethnic discrimination.

In 1973, a joint committee of the Legislature had recommended that the state's higher education system approximate the general ethnic composition of its high school graduates. In 1984, the legislature passed a resolution calling for the achievement of "full educational equity," now defined as proportionalism in terms of admissions *and* graduation rates. In 1989, another joint committee of the legislature beat the drum for "educational equity," recommending that "each segment of California public higher education shall strive to approximate by the year 2000" the ethnic composition of recent high school graduates. Throughout the two decades, of course, the institutions that make up the system (with the exception of the community colleges, which have open admissions) had zealously pursued affirmative action, admitting students on the basis of race and ethnicity. In the name of "educational equity," Assembly Bill No. 2150 would have put the state formally in favor of the exacting proportionalism that previous legislatures had merely encouraged through reports and other means.

The bill declared that "individuals from historically and currently underrepresented groups who seek to enter higher education continue to labor under a disadvantage with individuals from other groups because of disparities in high school preparation and college and university admission, transfer, retention, and graduation rates." As proof of this, the bill adduced an assortment of statistical disparities—in the levels of underrepresented students eligible for and enrolling in college; of those "transferring from community colleges to four-year colleges and universities"; and of those "completing degrees in community colleges and four-year colleges and universities." Notwithstanding the inherent weakness of this kind of evidence, the bill committed the state to remedying the disparities. The bill defined "educational equity" as occurring when "the composition of all individuals at all educational levels, from elementary school student bodies through college and university student bodies, as well as elementary school faculty and administrative ranks through college and university faculty and administrative ranks, encompasses the diversity of the state"—an ambitious, even otherworldly goal. Consistent with this definition of educational equity, the bill declared the state's intent that "each segment" of higher education "shall strive to approximate, by 2000, a diverse student body which mirrors the composition of recent high school graduates, both in first-year classes and subsequent college and university graduating classes, for individuals from historically and currently underrepresented" groups.

Contrary to the premises of those backing the bill, the reality of daily life is that racial and ethnic groups do not achieve equal outcomes, in education or elsewhere, for reasons that cannot be reduced merely to discrimination. All groups are underrepresented in some ways and overrepresented in others; Asians, for example, make up 2.9 percent of the workforce but are "underrepresented" in football and basketball and "overrepresented" in other endeavors, constituting 11 percent of the nation's physicians, 7.2 percent of our college professors, 6.7 percent of our natural scientists, and 6 percent of our mathematical and computer scientists.[4] Despite such facts, the authors of the legislation were dead serious about achieving its goal in the year 2000, and about doing so through means other than the development of policies that might enhance educational performance in the lower levels of the state's public educational system. The bill imposed on the governing boards of the University of California system the responsibility of ensuring that each school pursued proportionalism, providing that the performance of school administrators would be evaluated in terms of how they executed their "diversity and educational equity" responsibilities. The bill obscured its implications by never mentioning the term "preferences," or even "affirmative action," and of course steered entirely clear of the word "quota." Yet as Custred has said, "If we define a quota as a specific numerical proportion . . . designed to attain a specific outcome . . . which must be reached by a given date, with consequences for those in authority if the goal is not reached, then we have in [this bill] a graduation quota based on race and ethnicity and mandated by statute."[5] Such a quota might well have required double (or more) standards for academic assessment, and doubtless would have led to discrimination against persons said to be "overrepresented" in the university system—Asians, more than any other group.

Having seen in Assembly Bill 2150 an even more ghastly future for California higher education, Wood and Custred worried that a similar bill would become law under a different governor. The fact that No. 2150 had passed without debate in the legislature, and with hardly any notice in the California press, only intensified their concern. And then they discovered, as Wood puts it, that "the problem was metastasizing everywhere"—in public employment and contracting, especially, from the state level on down.

By 1992, Wood and Custred had grown more certain that the only way to address the problem was through a state constitutional amendment, which voters ultimately must approve. They had hoped to get an amendment on the November 1994

ballot, but time and political circumstance worked against
them. Under the California Constitution, two-thirds of both
houses of the legislature may propose an amendment, and in
August 1994, Republican lawmakers in the state Assembly
pushed an early version of CCRI. But with Democrats in control of both houses of the legislature, and the proposed
amendment drawing vigorous opposition from state civil
rights leaders and the public employee unions, the measure
died after a three-hour hearing. Fortunately, the state constitution also provides a process by which the people themselves
may propose an amendment by referendum—the strategy
Wood and Custred finally decided to pursue. "The only way,"
says Custred, "was to take it to the people."

The prospect of California's voting on CCRI in 1996 caught
the attention of Republican presidential aspirants, including
Governor Wilson, who endorsed CCRI early in 1995 and
then moved on several fronts to end affirmative action. To
begin with, Wilson issued an executive order eliminating all
state preferential treatment requirements lacking authoriza-
tion in state or federal law. In other words, he ended discretionary employment preferences, such as those adopted by
the water resources and the forestry and fire protection
departments under which a certain percentage of jobs were
reserved for women and minorities only. The executive order
also sought to conform state employment practices to the
Supreme Court's *Croson* decision by requiring that statuto-
rily required hiring goals be based on the percentages of
minorities in the qualified labor pool, not the percentages in
the work force generally. And the order eliminated one of the
subtle pressures of the affirmative action culture—a requirement that a hiring supervisor explain in writing why a
non–affirmative action candidate was hired if an "underrepresented" candidate was in the hiring pool.

Wilson also filed suit challenging the constitutionality of five state laws that encourage or require preferential treatment, all of which concern employment and contracting. When measured against the Supreme Court's 1989 *Croson* decision, these statutes had obvious infirmities. The laws requiring set-asides for minorities in contracting, for example, contained no findings of actual discrimination, as *Croson* demands. What is politically notable is that the legislature made little effort to bring these wayward statutes into conformity with *Croson,* nor did enforcement officials aware of *Croson* have much luck with their reform efforts. The director of affirmative action for the state's civil service system had recommended in 1993 that the basis for establishing hiring goals be changed from the percentage of minorities in the adult working population to the percentage with the requisite job qualifications. The proposed change wasn't made, however, because leaders of groups representing minorities and women objected on the ground it would dilute affirmative action efforts. California, of course, isn't the only state resisting *Croson,* but Wilson's lawsuit suggests the kind of effort it might take to prod a state to follow the Court's ruling.

Finally, Wilson used his position as head of the Board of Regents of the University of California to persuade majorities to end the use of preferences in admissions and faculty and staff hiring. Under the previous policy, in force since the 1970s, the university had made race such a "plus" in admissions as to effectively overturn the holding in the landmark *Bakke* case. As a result, Asians as well as whites were bearing the brunt of the system's discriminatory admissions policies. For example, as noted in chapter 4, the mean SAT score for whites and Asians admitted to the University of California at Berkeley was more than 200 points higher than those for Hispanics and blacks. And, according to a Pacific Research Institute study of admissions to the five University of California medical schools, minorities from nondisadvantaged backgrounds were being admitted over better qualified, disadvantaged Asians and whites.[6]

CCRI would make permanent the new, no-preference policy adopted by the University of California regents. A new board of regents thus would not be able to revive preferences in admissions (or hiring) unless the California Constitution first were changed. CCRI would similarly lock into place the no-preference policy Wilson established through executive order. But CCRI would reach further than Wilson could, outlawing not only every preference required or encouraged by a state statute or regulation in the areas of employment, education, and contracting, but all those sponsored by cities, counties, and other political subdivisions within the state.

A heated debate over CCRI erupted even before the drive to put it on the ballot began. The less incendiary opponents of CCRI have contended that the initiative is an extreme solution to problems created by affirmative action that instead should be dealt with on a case-by-case basis. Given the legislature's refusal to reconsider affirmative action programs, and the attachment of so many local governments to preferences, there would appear little prospect for a case-by-case reconsideration of affirmative action, at least not for one that would bring most preferences to an end. Even so, these opponents of the initiative argue that the California constitution should not flatly deny state and local governments the discretion to take race or sex into account, since unusual circumstances may arise in which preferences are needed.

This is a common argument against colorblind law, and the case often cited in the debate in California (as elsewhere) is that of a police department serving a racially mixed community: in order to perform effectively, it should not be prohibited from using preferences to hire and promote minority officers if race-neutral selection procedures fail to produce enough of them. The "operational needs" rationale, however, is a dangerous one. In 1993, a federal appeals court rebuked the chief of police in Charlotte, North Carolina, for relying on the operational-needs argument in promoting black officers less qualified than their white counterparts, and thus discriminating against the latter. (There were 74 candidates for 21 positions; when race-neutral selection procedures yielded one black among the top 21, the chief of police promoted three black officers ranking No. 29, No. 62, and No. 74, respectively.) Aware that segregationists in the 1950s and 1960s had cited "operational needs" to justify confining blacks to certain jobs, the court said that "we fear others could use this same rationale for a much less benign purpose. Such a result would promote racial polarization and the stereotypical view that only members of the same race can police themselves."[7]

As the long fight for colorblind law shows, governments have proved quite capable of coming up with rationales for classifying individuals on the basis of race. The question that CCRI ultimately poses is whether any of these rationales is strong enough to warrant preferential treatment—discrimination, by any other name. The Supreme Court has been correctly unimpressed by most of the justifications for preferences, though in the *Croson* case the Court indicated that it might be willing to accept preferences where "necessary to break down patterns of deliberate exclusion" of blacks, Hispanics, and other groups. But "deliberate exclusion" is hardly the issue in California, and if it ever becomes one, the answer is to correct the program or circumstances creating the exclusion, not to use race to deliberately exclude someone else from the opportunity to compete.

The real issue in California is preferential affirmative action. That is why CCRI is on the ballot. The measure would outlaw preferences regardless of their rationales. It would in effect adopt Justice Antonin Scalia's formulation of the issue in his *Adarand* opinion: that "government can never have a 'compelling interest' in discriminating on the basis of race in order to 'make up' for past racial discrimination in the opposite direction."

If California were its own nation, CCRI would more or less install colorblind governance throughout its territory. But, of course, California is a state whose governments and people are bound by federal statutes and the U.S. Constitution. CCRI thus cannot end within its borders preferential programs based on federal law. That is why California and other states seeking to end affirmative action cannot achieve that goal entirely on their own. Ending affirmative action will require decisions at the federal level.

The New Congress and the Clinton Response

In the first weeks of the new Congress, two House Republican committee chairmen—Henry Hyde of the Judiciary Committee and Bill Goodling of the Labor and Education Committee—said that they intended to hold hearings on the Clinton administration's enforcement of laws involving affirmative action, including the Justice Department's reversal in the *Piscataway* case. And then Bill Archer, chairman of the House Ways and Means Committee, moved to end a specific affirmative action program.

Viacom, the world's second largest entertainment media conglomerate, had decided to sell its cable television systems

to a man named Frank Washington. Owner of a company that
would provide 20 percent of the purchase price of $2.3 bil-
lion, Washington had secured the remainder from a private
investment firm. But the critical fact in the deal was that
Washington is black, and because Viacom was selling to a
"minority-led investor group," under rules established by the
Federal Communications Commission (FCC), Viacom would
have been permitted to defer indefinitely payment on more
than $1 billion in taxes. The deal was good for Viacom, but
the rationale behind the FCC policy was that the tax break
would allow the seller to offer at a lower-than-market price to
a minority-led investor group, thus giving the latter a break.
What the policy meant was that such buyers could enjoy a
substantial wealth increase by turning around and selling the
property, as was often done. On the assumption that Viacom's
cable holdings were being sold at roughly $200 million
below market price, Washington's firm was slated to enjoy an
increase in wealth approximately 20 percent of that, or $40
million. Washington, it turned out, was a millionaire who had
benefited from four other similar deals. To say he knew how
to work these deals is an understatement: as general counsel
at the FCC during the Carter administration, he had helped
craft the policy, dubiously justified on the ground that the
views of racial minorities are inadequately represented in the
broadcast media—the theory being that a minority-owned
station would offer more minority programming than a non-
minority-owned station would. (There was never any good
evidence to support this theory; the argument indulged in
the racialist stereotype which holds that there is such a thing
as a minority and a nonminority viewpoint—that, to put it
bluntly, thinking itself is a function of skin color.[8]) In early
February, the Ways and Means Committee under Archer's

direction passed a proposal to repeal the FCC policy, the first step on a journey that ended later in the spring with the president reluctantly signing the legislation. Congress used the savings realized from ending this preference to pay for newly legislated health benefits for self-employed individuals and their families.

Later in February, the Congressional Research Service (CRS) responded to a request made by Senate Majority Leader Robert Dole for a list of all statutes, regulations, programs, and executive orders that extend preferences on account of race, ethnicity, or sex. The CRS produced a thirty-two-page list of approximately 160 federal preferences, most of which represent efforts to increase minority and female participation in contracting, federally assisted programs, and employment. The disease had indeed "metastasized," to use Tom Wood's term. According to the CRS study, the Labor Department's enforcement of numerical affirmative action upon federal contractors had proved to be the model for subsequent "goal-oriented" programs. The Small Business Administration's set-aside policy had shaped still other federal preference programs. In sum, preferences were now either required or encouraged in a wide variety of programs—agriculture, banking, commerce, communications, defense, education, energy, the environment, health and human services, housing and urban development, justice, labor, foreign affairs, transportation, and veterans affairs, among others. Dole aides began writing legislation that would end preferences in federal programs, while Dole himself, joined by fellow GOP presidential aspirants Phil Gramm and Lamar Alexander, spoke out against preferential affirmative action.

In the months following the midterm election, President Clinton had not addressed affirmative action, his aides wrestling among themselves and with him over what he should do. *U.S. News and World Report* reported on February 13 that the administration seemed "sluggish, even paralyzed" over the issue. The reason was obvious: the majority of Americans were to the right of the administration on affirmative action, yet if Clinton were to move in their direction, he risked alienating the "groups" and their champions in Congress. Already Charles Rangel, the New York Democrat, upset over the Ways and Means Committee vote against the FCC's tax certificate policy, had issued an inflammatory statement comparing the racial attitudes of House Republicans to Adolf Hitler's and condemning their action as a move against poor minorities. Rangel's response seemed excessive, to say the least, and hard to explain, given that the FCC program had benefited even wealthy celebrities, such as Julius Erving, Mr. T, and O. J. Simpson. But when Archer strongly objected to the Hitler comparison, Rangel replied in a letter in which he made clear his belief that any effort to end affirmative action, even affirmative action for the wealthy, was an attack upon all blacks. The message to Clinton was clear. If he were to take initiative against federal affirmative action programs, he risked not only sharp criticism from those in his own party who agreed with Rangel, but also their disaffection and alienation as 1996 drew near. The last thing the Clinton White House wanted was a primary challenge from Jesse Jackson, a recipe for weakening and perhaps destroying Clinton's presidency.

Clinton knew he could not join the Republicans in moving against affirmative action, yet he could not simply announce a stout defense of the status quo. Obviously, he had to do something or risk irrelevance. In late February, he opted for a strategy designed, as one aide says, "to buy time," when he asked senior White House adviser George Stephanopoulos to conduct an "intense, urgent review" of all federal affirmative action programs. Even this decision required public explanation. "We shouldn't be defending things that we can't defend," said Clinton. "So it's time to review it, discuss it, and be straightforward about it." The news of the review lifted New Democrat hopes that Clinton might make midcourse corrections of the policies symbolized by the Justice Department's reversal in the *Piscataway* case. But the very idea of a review drew a sharp dissent from Jackson, who said Democrats should be "standing up and defending" one of the nation's "great success stories rather than having it turned into a wedge."

White House aides told the press that the review would be completed in a few weeks. But March became April, and April turned into May, and the review, conducted by Stephanopoulos and Christopher Edley, a Harvard law professor, was not completed. Still, there seemed little doubt that eventually Clinton would come out strongly in favor of most if not all federal affirmative action programs.

If Clinton himself were ever unsure about what he had to do, he had his feet repeatedly held to the fire. Jackson and other pro–affirmative action civil rights leaders advised him in person and through the news media. So did a newly formed coalition of liberal feminist groups, aware that Clinton had been advised to drop women from the list of groups favored by affirmative action. For his part, Senator Christopher Dodd, chairman of the Democratic National Committee, said that ending affirmative action would be "a huge mistake," adding that he defied anyone "to find a single regulation that talks about quotas." House Minority Leader Richard Gephardt also defended affirmative action in its current form, blasting the idea floated by New Democrats of basing affirmative action on economic need instead of race or sex. Responding to the insistent liberal message, administration officials let it be known every few weeks that there would be "no retreat" on affirmative action.

On July 19, the White House released the Edley-Stephanopoulos review, with the president strongly defending affirmative action in a speech delivered at the National Archives to a sympathetic audience that included numerous civil rights activists. The 97-page review concluded that federal affirmative action programs "worked" and were "fair." While allowing that reforms would make some programs work better and ensure their fairness, the review did not recommend the elimination of any of them. "We were able to deliver an uncluttered message," says Stephanopoulos. The president carried out the only recommendation Edley and Stephanopoulos made — that he tell agency heads to examine their programs in light of four "basic policy principles" the president had devised during the review and with reference to the Supreme Court's June 12 decision in *Adarand*.

The four principles did not promise to alter the status quo. Though one principle held that affirmative action should not go on forever, the administration, having spent five months reviewing federal programs, had been unable to find a single one it could end. Another principle said that there should be "no quotas," and yet there were quotas left untouched. For example, the Defense Department, under the Rule of Two, was setting aside contracts for minorities whenever two or more minority-owned businesses were bidding for a contract. A third principle held that there should be "no reverse discrimination." The affirmative action review explained: "Two wrongs don't make a right. Illegal discrimination includes reverse discrimination; reverse discrimination is discrimination, and it is wrong." So far, so good, but then the review added: "Affirmative action, when done right, is not reverse discrimination." In other words, preferential treatment is not necessarily reverse discrimination. With this "principle," the administration could make words mean whatever it wanted them to mean. As for the remaining principle—that there should be "no preferences for unqualified individuals"—it begged the question: What about programs that prefer less qualified individuals over those more qualified? That is the usual issue. Rarely is anyone absolutely unqualified for the opportunity in question.

Unlike the president's policy principles, the *Adarand* decision plainly threatened the status quo. Most federal preferences were originally rationalized in terms of statistics and anecdotes suggesting nothing more specific than societal discrimination, and yet, as the Justice Department's Walter Dellinger acknowledged in a memo to administration officials, such material "would not [under *Adarand*] be a sufficient predicate for a remedial racial or ethnic classification."[9] But the administration's so-called *Adarand* review obviously did not promise to lead to the wholesale elimination of preferences. Not only did the president's policy instincts lie in the entirely opposite direction, but his lawyers, who had argued for a different result in *Adarand*, naturally disagreed with the Court's ruling. Deval Patrick indicated the depth of their disagreement when he said that the administration would not be intimidated by *Adarand*.

The political significance of the president's "uncluttered" position on affirmative action could not be missed. In the short run, the president had pleased a core constituency within his own party and averted a primary challenge from Jesse Jackson. And, if a lawsuit subsequently compelled the administration to end a preferential program, it could plausibly say to that constituency that *Adarand* had forced its hand.

The New Democrats' Response

President Clinton's response to the question of what to do about affirmative action revealed a politician oddly stuck in the past who had learned nothing since the 1960s and who was unable to fathom the heart of the issue. Clinton held the confident belief of the Johnson-era bureaucrats who thought that government could regulate by race to an unambiguously good effect. Like those bureaucrats, he saw affirmative action as a mainly black issue, displaying no understanding of the quarter-century impact of immigration upon affirmative action. Somehow, Clinton had managed to persuade himself not only that most complaints about affirmative action were unmerited but also that two decades of hard economic times for middle-class white males explained those complaints—this was, he told the state Democratic Convention in California, "a psychologically tough time for white males." Thus, in Clinton's mind, was the controversy over affirmative action explained away. Nor did Clinton recognize that Americans neither white nor male have concerns about preferences. According to an October 1995 survey sponsored by the *Washington Post,* Harvard University, and the Kaiser Foundation, huge majorities of blacks, Hispanics, and Asians oppose using race even as "a factor in college admissions or employment."[10] Other surveys showed large majorities of women continuing to oppose preferences.[11] Finally, not once did Clinton question the use of race that preferential treatment entails, not even in the context of saying that it is a dubious means we must embrace for awhile. He did not express concern about the invitation to think in racial terms—and stereotypes—that affirmative action extends. To him, apparently, race was not as dangerous as fire: it can be played with safely.

Clinton's reaffirmation of the status quo drew a dissent from the Democratic Leadership Council (DLC), which faulted the President for "failing to address the public's doubts about the basic fairness of race-conscious policies." In a statement of its position, the DLC was wise where Clinton was not: it recognized the relevance of immigration to the affirmative action debate; it did not patronize white males; it took seriously the discrimination that results from preferential treatment; and it clearly understood the problem posed to our civic culture by affirmative action, namely, that it "divides Americans most dramatically along racial lines," making it "more rather than less difficult to transcend racial difference." On this last point, the statement (written by Will Marshall) was especially insightful: "Reducing the significance of race, looking beyond the color of our skin to our common humanity—this, after all, was the essence of Dr. Martin Luther King's celebrated dream. . . . Dr. King's moral vision, not the current push for race-conscious preferences and group entitlements, remains the surest lodestar for a society still struggling to overcome the traumatic legacy of racial subjugation."[12]

Though the DLC supported preferences in private employment and in higher education admissions, it did speak to the issue now at the heart of the debate in Washington by recommending that preferences in all federal programs, including employment, should be phased out. The organization offered two compelling reasons: preferences contradict the principle of equal treatment for all, and they "put government in the business of institutionalizing racial distinctions, hardly a good idea for a democracy held together only by

common civic ideals that transcend group identity." The DLC
thus endorsed the notion of a colorblind federal government.

Although the DLC presented its differences with the Clinton administration as minor, they were anything but that. The
willingness of the DLC to "separate race and state," as the
organization declared should be done, borrowing an idea
advanced by *The Economist* magazine, contrasted sharply with
Clinton's rejection of colorblind law. Also, the organization
explicitly disagreed with the Clinton administration over the
future of the government's largest affirmative action program—the "goals and timetables" regime imposed on federal
contractors by the Labor Department in enforcing Executive
Order 11246. The DLC bluntly recommended that the program be repealed, offering this realistic assessment: "Although
the law bans formal quotas, government guidelines push
employers to hire by the numbers to avoid the inference of
discrimination." The Clinton administration, in defending the
program, went so far as to deny that the guidelines ever push
contractors toward preferences. Moreover, Shirley Wilcher,
Clinton's director of the Office of Federal Contract Compliance Programs, as it is now called, told Congress that if contractors passed over a more qualified person in favor of a less
qualified one in order to satisfy the OFCCP, such contractors
would be in violation of the executive order. Wilcher thus
maintained that the OFCCP does not require or encourage or
even allow preferences—a statement that, if true, would mark
a historic change in the way the program has been administered. Of course, there has been no such change. In the summer of 1995, a federal contractor in Florida discovered that
race- and sex-neutral procedures for laying off employees in
part of its workforce had failed to produce the "right" numbers. In response, said the affirmative action manager, "We'd

massage the numbers to make sure there wasn't a dispropor-
tionate representation of females and minorities in the bottom
of the relative ranking."[13] In other words, the company resorted
to preferences in order to satisfy the OFCCP.

The best explanation for Wilcher's completely implausible
testimony was desperation to save the program she administers from the new legal standards set out in *Adarand*. The
problem may well be insuperable: for more than twenty
years, the OFCCP's numerical enforcement has been rationalized as a way to overcome "societal discrimination"—a
rationale that the Supreme Court repeatedly has rejected.

The Republicans Raise the Stakes

On July 27, 1995, Senator Robert Dole and Representative
Charles T. Canady formally unveiled legislation addressing
affirmative action at the federal level. Like the California
Civil Rights Initiative, the bill sharply distinguishes between
affirmative action understood in terms of nondiscriminatory
recruitment and outreach, on the one hand, and preferential
affirmative action on the other. It proposes to save the former
and end the latter. Specifically, it would eliminate preferences in the employment practices of the federal government
and also in the awarding of prime contracts. Further, it would
prevent government from requiring or encouraging prime
contractors to prefer a subcontractor on the basis of race or
sex. The bill would also end preferences in the administration of all other federal programs, including the OFCCP's
enforcement of Executive Order 11246.

The bill specifies that the government may not grant a
preference to any individual or group "based in whole or in

part on race, color, national origin, or sex." (Like CCRI, the legislation recognizes that there is no separate case for preferences based on gender.) The language "in whole or in part" covers the use of race or sex as "a factor"—the favored formula of those who believe, wrongly, that race or sex is not the determining factor so long as it is only one of many factors. The bill exhaustively defines "a preference" as a quota, set-aside, numerical goal, timetable, or other numerical objective. It also defines the term to include any use of race or sex—even one not tied to a numerical goal—to favor one person over another.

The Dole-Canady bill is the wiser for the experience of thirty years of affirmative action. It reflects the understanding that it is not enough to oppose "quotas," as Republicans have in the past, as if the rigid nature of a quota, or its label, is somehow its central offense. The authors of the bill also were wise to the tricks of the affirmative action bureaucracy, which long ago swore off quotas, at least publicly, and resorted to a variety of other devices, all of which, at the end of the day, use race or sex to determine who gets an opportunity and who doesn't.

Like the California Civil Rights Initiative, the bill was written on the understanding that the principle of nondiscrimination must protect *everyone*. Though the framers of civil rights legislation in the 1950s and 1960s believed that the principle of nondiscrimination was universal in its application, the practice of affirmative action quickly required qualification of that principle if some persons were to be preferred over others on account of race or sex. Thus the Dole-Canady bill provides that no one in government, nor any agency of government, may discriminate against "any individual or group" on account of race, color, national origin, or sex. In this same provision, the bill prohibits *favoring* "any individual or group" on these

grounds. Thus, the legislation takes aim at what we know, by any other name, is discrimination.

The Dole-Canady bill does not touch Titles VI or VII of the Civil Rights Act of 1964, but ending preferential affirmative action will require changes in the way both have been implemented, making explicit the illegality of favoring or disfavoring someone on the basis of race. The original colorblind constraints of Title VI have been loosened through regulation, allowing recipients of federal money (such as private universities) to "take race into account" in allocating limited opportunities. And the deformation of Title VII wrought by the federal judiciary has increased the potential for discrimination on the basis of race and sex in private and public employment.

Some writers and scholars have recently argued that Title VII should apply to the public sector but not the private sector. The argument has little political prospect, but because it has become part of the public debate, it cannot be ignored. The argument is this: while public employers are accountable to the public and should be bound by the nondiscrimination principle, private employers are not accountable to the public and therefore should have the freedom to hire or not hire whomever they want, for whatever reason. Market forces would reduce irrational discrimination while rewarding discrimination that is economically efficient—so-called rational discrimination. This argument puts economic values ahead of nondiscrimination. But the argument is unpersuasive. The original Title VII sought to focus the attention of private employers entirely on the merits of the individuals that they might hire or promote. The law did so by absolutely excluding race from the definition of job qualifications. That judgment remains the right one. Our nation's history counsels that protecting individuals against racial discrimination ought to rank above ensuring maximum economic efficiency. We have learned that there are costs to discrimination that can't be put in economic terms. Race is a potentially toxic element in our society, and the Congress that passed Title VII was wise to put it off limits to private employers.

A somewhat different argument for lifting Title VII from the private sector maintains that what is natural should be legal: that is, because it is natural for members of a particular racial or ethnic group to prefer people of that group, the law should allow them to discriminate in favor of their own. Thus, Asians should be able to hire Asians, as should blacks and, to push the argument to its logical conclusion, also whites. This particular argument, advanced by Dinesh D'Souza in his 1995 book *The End of Racism,* would permit discrimination in the name of ethnocentrism.[14] This argument, too, is wrong. Korean-owned grocery stores may well want to hire mainly Koreans (the example D'Souza gives), but one reason we had a civil rights movement was to prevent the claims of the tribe or clan from blunting the aspirations of the individual. Employers with fewer than fifteen employees are exempt from Title VII, not as a tribute to ethnocentrism but for reasons of practicality: there are limits to what government can enforce.

The problem with Title VII is not its private-sector coverage but its deformation in the hands of judges and bureaucrats. The urgency is to make sure that Title VII, applying to both the public and private sector, means what it originally said: no discrimination against any person on account of race or sex. Thus, new law could prohibit courts and law enforcement agencies from interpreting Title VII to require, encourage, or permit the use of preferences. It could also make clear that operational needs, customer relations, diversity, inclusion, and the like may not justify favoring one person over another on account of race or sex.

Today, of course, the issue before the country does not involve Title VI or Title VII but the federal government itself. The focus is a natural one, especially given that the Supreme Court's decision in the *Adarand* case extends beyond preferences in federal contracting to those in all federal programs. And while other like-minded bills were proposed in Congress in 1995—Representative Gary Franks proposed one that would end preferences in contracting only—the Dole-Canady legislation is the most comprehensive.

The Recovery of Colorblind Law

During the balance of 1995, with Republicans holding hearings on their legislation, the administration continued to review federal programs in light of the president's four policy principles and the *Adarand* decision. But by the end of the year, the administration had not announced any change in any federal program resulting from this review. As we saw in chapter 6, the Defense Department did end the Rule of Two, but only as a result of a lawsuit challenging the procedure. Committed to preserving the status quo and aware of the vulnerability of so many federal programs containing preferences, the administration undertook a massive effort at a cost of $1.7 million to find evidence of discrimination that might provide legal support for these programs. Of course, any effort to develop at the federal level the "solid basis in evidence" that the Court now requires promises to be very difficult, if not impossible. And there is the related question of whether, in any event, the Court will accept such "after-the-fact" evidence. But these considerable problems did not

deter the administration from trying to shore up constitu-
tionally dubious programs.

Consistent with this effort, the administration also
announced its opposition to the Dole-Canady bill, as Deval
Patrick told a House committee in December that the attorney general would strongly recommend a presidential veto.
In his testimony, Patrick vigorously defended the use of race
or sex as "one factor among others" in allocating opportunities and the use of numerical goals, even though (as we have
seen) race or sex is never merely "a factor" but the determining factor, and numerical goals inevitably result in preferential treatment. Patrick traded in the standard euphemisms of
affirmative action, while suggesting that the legislation would
set back integration.

Patrick's testimony left to congressional Republicans the
next move, which they could take in 1996. But the leadership
may have weak knees. Although Republicans control both
houses of Congress, few in their ranks understand the affirmative action issue well or are able to argue it intelligently.
Indeed, the party is divided over how, and how rapidly, to
proceed in ending affirmative action, or even whether to end
it at all.

The rifts within the GOP were revealed over the course of
1995. Some Republicans, like Jack Kemp, held to a view not
unlike Clinton's. "I think race is a legitimate factor to take
into consideration," Kemp told the *Washington Post*. Others,
like Franks, one of two black Republicans in Congress,
opposed preferences in contracting but not in employment.
Still others, most prominently House Speaker Newt Gingrich, professed agreement in principle with the Dole-Canady
legislation. But Gingrich opposed moving the legislation
through Congress in 1995, citing the congested legislative
calendar. The deeper reason, however, was that Gingrich

believed it necessary to develop an adequate "replacement" policy—"the second half," as he called it—which would signal to blacks the party's good faith. "It's important for us to say we are for inclusion," he said, and that Republicans not "send a message of being insensitive to or hostile to minorities who are trying to rise." Driving replacement-policy efforts was fear of the kind of attack launched against House Republicans earlier in the year by Charles Rangel—an attack that has long proved effective. "We need to address affirmative action without being accused of being racist," said Representative Jack Kingston of Georgia, displaying his sensitivity to such accusations. Others, such as Senator Phil Gramm of Texas, hoped to win quick victories by attaching antipreference riders to other bills—a controversial legislative approach that went nowhere. Meanwhile, several of the party's presidential contenders competed among themselves, it seemed, to secure the anti–affirmative action vote in 1996. Kemp discerned an attempt to use affirmative action as a "wedge" issue to win the election—a strategy he said he would not be party to. Sadly, in the run-up before the election year, none of the presidential contenders seemed to understand that ending affirmative action is more than a campaign issue. It cuts to the very heart of what the nation is about.

Given this picture of a party in conflict over how and when to proceed on affirmative action, it was far from certain in early 1996 that the Republican Congress would pass any legislation by the end of the year on an issue that had been placed on the national agenda by the election that brought it to power. The issue, however, shows no signs of going away. And it is entirely possible that the California Civil Rights Initiative and the formation of a third party, if that occurs, could play key roles in the endgame of affirmative action and the recovery of our best principles as a people. CCRI, if approved by a substantial margin, could stimulate similar ballot measures in the 23 states with an initiative process, leading to a widespread movement for nondiscrimination that might embolden congressional Republicans, joined by moderate Democrats, finally to pass legislation like the Dole-Canady bill. Alternatively, such a movement could find its home in a new political party, something already on the minds of many Americans, including some leading Republicans and Democrats. The presence of such a party could help in the recovery of colorblind law, especially if it understands and advances a vision of America that is rooted in the Declaration of Independence and its embrace of equal rights for all individuals.

9

Ending Affirmative Action

One of the central and hard-won lessons of the fight for colorblindness, lasting more than a century and a quarter, was that distinctions drawn on the basis of race inevitably lead to racial discrimination. That is why the advocates of colorblindness sought the elimination of racial distinctions in the law. They sought to end the source, the raw material, of racial discrimination. The nation was the better for their efforts when, starting in the 1940s, our legal system was strengthened by the addition of a variety of antidiscrimination laws, culminating in the Civil Rights Act of 1964. Soon afterward, the founders of affirmative action, searching for ways to improve the material condition of black Americans and make amends for slavery and segregation, found the constraints of colorblind law inconvenient. They managed to loosen the colorblind strictures of the Civil

Rights Act of 1964, and the federal judiciary failed to tighten
them in turn. Once preferential treatment was made possible, it spread throughout the public and private sectors, and
the targets of numerical affirmative action became more
numerous, coming to include Hispanics, Asians, and women.

Defenders of the policy initially promised that it would be
temporary—a position that implicitly recognized that it is
better not to sort people on the basis of race, that colorblindness is a worthy guide. But with the first step away from
colorblindness, further steps came more easily, and in time
we heard less often the promise that someday we would
renew our previous commitment.

Nonetheless, more than a quarter century of thinking by
race and counting by race has served only to confirm and
strengthen the case for colorblind law.

We now know that when government has the power to
sort people on the basis of race, racial discrimination often
results. Preferential treatment is never benign. Whoever
would have been admitted to a school, or won the promotion
or the contract, but for race, has suffered discrimination—
and there is no good discrimination. The nation owes a debt
of gratitude to people like Allan Bakke, Brian Weber, Randy
Pech, and Cheryl Hopwood, who have brought lawsuits challenging preferential affirmative action. They have coura-
geously kept alive the question of the legality and morality of
preferential treatment, providing often lonely witness to the
principle at the heart of colorblind law—that no one in
America should be discriminated against on account of race.

We know, too, that the effort to regulate on the basis of
race can have unanticipated consequences. Where the old
advocates of colorblind law were pessimists about the very
idea of racial regulation, the founders of affirmative action
were optimists, confident of their ability to distinguish

between benign and invidious racial classifications. They thought the world could be divided into good and bad people. The bad discriminated against blacks, either intentionally or through seemingly neutral procedures that produced adverse effects. The good—and the founders of affirmative action included themselves in this category—sought to do well by blacks. They were pure in heart, and so they could be trusted not to harm blacks.

But now we know better. It was weak-minded and dangerously naive to think that taking race into account would produce unambiguously good results for those in whose behalf it was done. Many ostensible beneficiaries of affirmative action have testified that preferential treatment often leads to self-doubt, dependency, and entitlement. To be sure, affirmative action doesn't always do that. Sometimes it "works," though the paradox of affirmative action is that its "working" is a function of how soon the recipient quits it entirely and labors under the same rules as everyone else, a sign of genuine equality that is possible only among individuals. But, as the practice of affirmative action has shown, no one knows enough confidently to predict in advance of an act of preferential treatment which effects, for better or worse, it will have upon a given recipient. This negative experience of affirmative action does not constitute an unanswerable argument against it; patients do undergo risky operations. But we do have a choice in the matter; that is, we do not have to take the risk of affirmative action. And once free of it, those now eligible for it would be able to compete and achieve on the same terms as everyone else.

There have been other unanticipated consequences as well, chief among them the stigma produced by affirmative action. Wherever affirmative action operates, the very existence of such a program will lead some people to think that every minority student or every minority employee would not have won opportunity without preferential treatment, a judgment that strips people of the respect due them as individuals. Consider, in the context of higher education, the case of the minority student admitted under affirmative action who would not have won the place without it. This student very well might have been admitted to another school, without the "help" of affirmative action. The problem, however, is that the student admitted under affirmative action is unable to erase its stigma until the individual succeeds in a nonpreferential environment. Even then, however, the number of those who know the nature of the student's achievement is likely to be very small. And the formal, pervasive nature of affirmative action, encouraged and required by so many local, state, and federal government agencies, means that the public will continue to make generalizations about minority advancement simply because it is easy to do so in the absence of particular knowledge. The generalization is that "minority" equals "affirmative action" equals "lower standards." The inference drawn is that affirmative action explains minority success. Tragically, this process of generalization and inference trails the many minorities—perhaps the majority—who make their way without the "help" of any preferential treatment.

Here the negative experience of affirmative action makes a powerful argument for colorblind law. Because affirmative action is stigmatizing, even for those who do not "benefit" from it, it is better to forego affirmative action altogether in favor of procedures for admitting students or hiring workers or awarding contracts that do not brand their targets as inferior and do not provide a basis for generalizing about minority achievement. Such procedures, of course, are those that do not distinguish on the basis of race, that do not "take race into account" in deciding who gets ahead.

Sports, fortunately, is still a world governed by such color-blind rules. No one receives preferential treatment in sports, so no one has self-doubts induced by affirmative action, no one has to "transcend" affirmative action, and no one is stigmatized by affirmative action. No one ever thinks, "Williams is in center field because of affirmative action," or "Lopez is catching because he is Hispanic." Outside of sports—which is to say, in the rest of society—the deeply human desire to be known for individual accomplishment explains why some minorities have made a point of declining participation in programs for which their race or ethnicity makes them eligible. The Hispanic law student at the University of Texas School of Law, whose academic qualifications were good enough to be admitted under the standards governing "white and others," was making an important point when he said that sometimes he wished he was wearing a shirt indicating his academic credentials. Ending affirmative action will create circumstances in which individuals will shine and, just as importantly, be seen to shine, quite on their own merits.

The longer affirmative action remains in place, the more reasons there are to bring it to an end. Of course, past advocates of colorblind law could have told us how hard it would be to quit thinking and counting by race once the racial license had been granted. They knew that the human mind is creative, remarkably capable of coming up with reasons, even quite attractive ones, for why we ought to "take race into account." The founding rationale of affirmative action was to remedy the ill effects of past discrimination against blacks, but this rationale did not easily fit the other groups. So affirmative action was redefined and rejustified in terms of overcoming "underrepresentation" and achieving "diversity." We have also heard the argument that affirmative action is necessary to prevent future discrimination. There have been other reasons offered: affirmative action is needed to create minority role models, to stimulate the creation of minority businesses, to jump-start economic development in minority communities. With the advent at the local level of minority-dominated governments, minorities have discriminated against nonminorities by fashioning affirmative action programs that, while publicly touted in terms of one or another of the usual rationales, realistically are little more than expressions of racial politics, the ignoble triumph of minority majorities.

The use of race now threatens to produce some truly bizarre results. In large cities where new immigrants congregate, blacks who hold disproportionately more public-sector jobs stand to lose some of those jobs to "underrepresented" Hispanics. Diversity, meanwhile, is a rationale that may allow discrimination against members of traditional minority groups. Even President Clinton has said he would support laying off a black teacher instead of a white teacher if doing so would promote diversity. We cannot escape the fact that by drawing racial and ethnic lines, affirmative action—whatever its rationale—encourages Americans to think of themselves in racial and ethnic terms. That has been a recipe for resentment and chauvinism, neither of which promotes the good health of our democracy.

Fortunately, the Supreme Court has kept the light on, letting us know where home is, even in those cases where it has ruled in support of affirmative action. Those justices of the Supreme Court who consistently voted for affirmative action programs nonetheless refused to endorse group rights or to break in principle with the colorblind tradition. Equality under the Constitution, Justice Brennan wrote, is linked "with the proposition that differences in color or creed, birth or status, are neither significant nor relevant to the way in

which such persons are treated." Justice Marshall declared
his desire to live in a society "in which the color of a person's
skin will not determine the opportunities available to him or
her." And Justice Blackmun endorsed a society in which
"persons will be regarded as persons," without regard to race
or ethnicity.[1]

In recent years the Court has been shining the home light
much more brightly. Its decisions in the *Croson* and *Adarand*
cases, which speak to every government in the United States,
impose strict conditions on the use of racial preferences.
These decisions point us in the right direction. Citing Justice
Harlan's dissent in *Plessy* v. *Ferguson* and the opinions in the
Japanese Relocation Cases, *Croson* and *Adarand* raise the
standard of colorblind law in a context that makes colorblindness even more compelling today than Harlan could
have known. He made his argument for colorblind law in the
context of a society made up of two races—black and white.
Ours today consists of many races and ethnic groups, thanks
especially to recent waves of immigration. Law that tries to
distinguish among the groups and to favor one over another
is bound to fail the country. Instead, we need law that can
discourage the natural tendency people have to seek their
own kind, law that invites people to minimize and transcend
racial and ethnic differences. The best protection for every
individual—of whatever race or ethnic background—is to be
found in law that does not give effect to any racial views, but,
as Harlan put it, provides for "equality before the law of all
citizens of the United States, without regard to race."

The Supreme Court, however, has left much of the task of
ending affirmative action to the American people.[2] That is
just as well. Decisions by the elective branches of government to end programs containing preferences would be
reached consequent to public debate, not after legal briefs

have been submitted. We can take major steps toward recovering colorblind law and principle by enacting measures at the federal and state levels that would deny government the power to favor or slight anyone on account of race. If we do not take such steps, of course, the uncertain political tides may turn back to favor the supporters of affirmative action. Progress toward colorblind law will be much slower, if not impossible, if we rely exclusively on judicial decisions, for the defenders of affirmative action will respond by "mending" programs in ways that better disguise preferences but do not eliminate them. It is possible, too, that judicial progress toward colorblind law could be arrested or even reversed, if there are new Supreme Court appointees with views at odds with those of the majorities in *Croson* and *Adarand*. It falls to us to take action now.

The choice for colorblindness is the choice our own best tradition invites us to make. Our founding charter declares that "all men are created equal" and are "endowed by their Creator with certain unalienable rights," among them "life, liberty, and the pursuit of happiness." We are thereby committed to the proposition that it is individuals who have rights, not groups, and that all individuals enjoy a fundamental equality of rights. The startling character of the United States—and what it has modeled to the rest of the world—is that the individuals who have equal rights may be of any race or ethnic background.

Few Americans have stated the case for equality as cogently as Abraham Lincoln, who did so in an 1858 speech he gave in Chicago in observation of Independence Day. The challenge before Lincoln was to show that the truths of the Declaration of Independence were relevant to the audience before him, which included European immigrants who were

not descended from those who wrote the Declaration, fought
the Revolution, and framed the Constitution. Having paid
honor to the "men living in that day whom we claim as our
fathers and grandfathers," and having linked the principle
they contended for to the nation's subsequent prosperity,
Lincoln told the audience that "we hold this annual celebra-
tion to remind ourselves of all the good done . . . and how it
was done and who did it, and how we are historically con-
nected with it." He added that "we go from these meetings in
better humor with ourselves—we feel more attached the one
to the other, and more firmly bound to the country we
inhabit." And, yes, those he was addressing were as much a
part of this country as anyone else:

> We have [besides those descended from the founders]
> . . . among us perhaps half our people who are not descen-
> dants at all of these men, they are men who have come
> from Europe—German, Irish, French and Scandinavian—
> men that have come from Europe themselves, or whose
> ancestors have come hither and settled here, finding them-
> selves our equals in all things. If they look back through
> this history to trace their connection with those days by
> blood, they find they have none, they cannot carry them-
> selves back into that glorious epoch and make themselves
> feel that they are part of us, but when they look through
> that old Declaration of Independence they find that those
> old men say that "We hold these truths to be self-evident,
> that all men are created equal," and then they feel that
> moral sentiment taught in that day evidences their relation
> to those men, that it is the father of all moral principle in
> them, and that they have a right to claim it as though they
> were blood of the blood, and flesh of the flesh of the men
> who wrote that Declaration, and so they are.[3]

As Lincoln reminds us, the Declaration included any person from anywhere—the Germans and Swedes and other Europeans whom Lincoln addressed, the slaves Lincoln freed, the Asians who began arriving on our shores just before the nation was about to rend itself in a civil war, the Hispanics from all parts of the globe, Englishmen, American Indians, Jews—in sum, everyone. The Declaration is the great leveler, teaching that the rights of one are the rights of all. It puts us all on the same footing, and it implies the necessity of colorblind law because only that kind of law fully respects the equal rights of all persons, as individuals.

Affirmative action has always been an aberration from our best principles. The time has come to end it.

Afterword to the Paperback Edition

As the 1996 election season got underway, it appeared certain to many observers that affirmative action would become a major issue in the presidential race. Senator Bob Dole, the Republican nominee, had proclaimed his opposition to race- and sex-based preferences by co-sponsoring legislation (with Rep. Charles Canady) prohibiting their use by the federal government. And he had endorsed the California Civil Rights Initiative (CCRI), on the fall ballot in California as Proposition 209, a proposal to ban preferences in state employment, education, and contracting. As his party's standard-bearer, the conventional wisdom went, surely Dole would not fail to force a debate over government-sponsored preferences by challenging the stands of President Bill Clinton, who had announced his opposition both to Dole-Canady and Proposition 209.

Had Dole drawn Clinton into this debate, and had Dole then been elected president, the nation would have effectively decided to eliminate preferential affirmative action on the part of government. Passage of a federal law banning preferences (like the Dole-Canady bill) would have been assured, especially given the voters' other decision on Election Day—to maintain Republican control of Congress. But of course events did not play out this way.

Dole decided not to take the offensive and remained silent on the issue of preferences during the spring and summer. There was a practical reason: Trying to recruit Colin Powell as his running mate, Dole did not wish to undermine that effort by emphasizing an issue on which Powell held views contrary to his. In early August, when Dole tapped Jack Kemp as his vice-presidential nominee, the result was a Republican ticket potentially at odds with itself, since Kemp had supported preferences as recently as 1995 and had declined to back the California Civil Rights Initiative. During the Republican National Convention Kemp tepidly endorsed the measure. His lack of enthusiasm for arguing against preferences also was evident during the October vice-presidential debate when he let pass without challenge Al Gore's remark that the Dole-Canady legislation and CCRI would "end all affirmative action." The response available to Kemp was the obvious one that these measures targeted only race- and sex-based preferences and thus would not disturb non-preferential affirmative action programs, such as those often used in recruiting and training workers. The division within the Republican ticket thus blunted the effectiveness of Dole's challenge to Clinton on the issue of preferences.

Dole made that challenge only intermittently, and then

usually in short passages in speeches touching on a variety of matters. The one speech devoted mostly to elaborating a case against preferences—a speech in California in behalf of CCRI—was arguably the best speech of Dole's campaign. It was a thoughtful, principled statement explaining why government should not make race a source of advantage or disadvantage when individuals are competing for limited seats in a university or jobs or contracts. But Dole made this speech only eight days before the election. Clinton, sitting on a big lead in the polls, had no reason to respond. In the absence of a strong, steady push commenced earlier in the year by a united Republican ticket, affirmative action never really became an issue of significance in the campaign.

For supporters of preferences, Clinton's re-election was one of the few bright spots of 1996, a year which saw judicial and political developments continuing to push against affirmative action.

In March, the Fifth Circuit Court of Appeals, ruling in *Hopwood* v. *Texas*, a case discussed at length in chapter 4, held that the University of Texas School of Law may not use race in selecting applicants for admission. In one respect, the decision represented merely an application of the antipreference doctrine that the Supreme Court has developed in recent years. But in another respect, the decision was pathbreaking, for it rejected the "diversity" rationale for admissions preferences set forth by Justice Lewis Powell in his well-known opinion in the 1978 *Bakke* case. Because diversity was the foundation on which the edifice of affirmative action in admissions had for so long been built, the Fifth Circuit's ruling sent shock waves through the world of higher education. The state of Texas, supported by a friend-of-the-court brief submitted by the Clinton Justice Department, asked the Supreme Court to review the decision, but the

Court declined. *Hopwood* is now the law for Texas, Louisiana, and Mississippi, the three states that comprise the Fifth Circuit.

In August, in the *Piscataway* case (discussed in chapter 5), the Third Circuit Court of Appeals upheld a district court's judgment that a New Jersey school board had discriminated against a white high school teacher by laying her off on account of race in order to satisfy its affirmative action plan. The Third Circuit's decision represented an emphatic refusal (the vote by the full panel was eight-to-four) to justify preferences in employment in terms of diversity. The ruling was also a rebuke to the Clinton administration, which, having successfully represented the white school teacher at trial, switched sides on appeal to argue that diversity is indeed a lawful basis for racial preferences.

The year also saw repeated defeats for municipalities trying to save preferential programs used in contracting. In the *Croson* case, which nullified a Richmond, Virginia, ordinance setting aside a certain percentage of contracts for minority-owned firms, the Supreme Court had specified that preferential policies must be based on specific, well-documented evidence of discrimination. As reported in chapter 6, many states and localities have responded to *Croson* by commissioning "disparity studies" in order to show that minorities aren't getting their "fair share" of public-works contracts. Lawsuits challenging the adequacy of such studies are starting to move through the federal courts, and in 1996 district courts in Miami and Columbus, Ohio, and the Third Circuit Appeals Court in Philadelphia, threw out new, post-*Croson* studies offered by local governments to sustain their policies.

But the biggest judgment against preferences in 1996 was rendered on Election Day in California, where more than 54 percent of the voters approved Proposition 209, an amendment to the state constitution. Soon thereafter, implementation of the measure began, as Governor Pete Wilson ordered new regulations eliminating preferences from state affirmative action programs, and the head of the University of California system announced the immediate end of preferences in admissions. Meanwhile, anti-preference groups in other states that had awaited the outcome on Proposition 209 energetically renewed their labors, especially in Washington, Oregon, Colorado, Florida, Georgia, North Carolina, Texas, Michigan, Illinois, Wisconsin, Ohio, Pennsylvania, New Jersey, and Massachusetts. All of these states but Texas have an initiative process whereby the people can bypass the ordinary political process and make law themselves.

Though these developments do not augur well for preferences, supporters of affirmative action have in Bill Clinton not only an ally but an elected official whose office is powerful enough to offer substantial defense. As president, Clinton can veto any legislation outlawing preferences in federal programs that the Republican Congress might pass. (During the 104th Congress, Clinton indicated his willingness to veto the Dole-Canady bill, which the Republican leadership decided to put over until 1997–1998.) Also, the Clinton Justice Department can file briefs in court cases in defense of local and state preferences, as it did in the *Hopwood* case.

Moreover, Clinton can continue to implement his policy, announced in the summer of 1995, of "mending, not ending" federal affirmative action programs. Under this policy, preferences faced little threat. Most were retained, and to justify preferences that might be attacked on the basis of the Supreme Court's 1995 decision in *Adarand*, which imposes sharp restrictions on the federal government's use of race, the administration collected local and state disparity studies and other materials that it could point to as evidence of discrimination that the federal preferences seek to "remedy." The year ended with the Justice Department defending preferences against a series of new challenges based on *Adarand*.

Finally, as he did in his first term, Clinton can appoint judges whose judicial philosophy inclines them to support preferences. Such judges will have more clout because their number will increase over the next four years and the number of judges named by Republican presidents, who generally work from a different judicial philosophy and are more skeptical toward preferences, will decline. By the end of his second term Clinton will have named half the sitting federal judiciary, but the critical question concerns the balance of power on the appeals courts, which, because so few of their decisions are actually reviewed by the Supreme Court, function as mini-Supreme Courts. Assuming the usual number of annual vacancies on those courts, appointees of Democratic presidents, who in general have proved more friendly toward preferences, could hold the balance of power in all but two of these courts. Moreover, if one of the seats on the Supreme Court now held by judicial conservatives is vacated, and Clinton names a liberal replacement, then the Court could conceivably weaken the doctrine against preferences it has written in the *Croson* and *Adarand* cases. In that event, the lower federal courts would be obligated to enforce Supreme Court doctrine more agreeable to preferences.

There are well-known constraints on the exercise of presidential power, such as the fact that the Republican-led Senate must vote to confirm the judges and justices Clinton nominates. Even so, given the constitutional authority Clinton uniquely has, and how it might be exercised, it's no wonder that soon after the election Jesse Jackson called on the president to lead a fight in behalf of affirmative action. Only because Clinton has proved so variable in his policy pursuits is it worth noting that he could once again decide to change directions on preferences and use the powers of his office to hasten their end. The more likely prospect, however, is that Clinton will remain on Jackson's side, fighting for preferences though probably not leading that fight on the terms Jackson demands.

One issue Clinton will face is whether the Justice Department should join the effort already underway to have Proposition 209 declared unconstitutional. Within hours after the vote on the measure had been counted, the American Civil Liberties Union commenced this legal battle by filing a lawsuit in federal court in San Francisco. One of the ACLU's two arguments is that Proposition 209 is unconstitutional because it conflicts with federal law, which the Constitution declares to be "the supreme law of the land." The authors of Proposition 209 included in the measure a subprovision permitting preferences in any instance in which eligibility for federal funds requires them. But the ACLU's argument goes beyond those circumstances to say that by forbidding preferences in all other circumstances Proposition 209 is at odds with federal law. Of course, there are statutes and other federal laws that allow and even encourage preferences, and it is true that in their enforcement some of these laws are seen to be coercive. But it is not obvious that federal law literally requires preferences. Only a judge trying to create a conflict where none exists would interpret federal law as indeed mandating them—and it is a rule of construction that judges should interpret statutes in such a fashion as to avoid having to make a constitutional judgment. The justices who currently hold the balance of power on the Supreme Court, should they be asked to do find a conflict between Proposition 209 and federal law, are unlikely to do so. Indeed, the conflict the current Court would more readily perceive is one between any federal statute said to require preferences and the Constitution, which it has interpreted as all but prohibiting government-sponsored preferences.

The ACLU's other contention is that, under the Fourteenth Amendment's equal protection clause, all citizens have a right to be able to participate in the political process "in a reliable and meaningful manner," but Proposition 209 violates this right by withdrawing from state and local officials the authority to enact programs that "inure to the benefit" of minorities and women. Supporters of race- and sex-based preferences can only argue for a new constitutional amendment to override Proposition 209, while supporters of other kinds of preferences (based on veteran's status, for example) are able to pursue their objectives through all of the ordinary political processes.

The "political participation" argument advanced by the ACLU relies on a 1982 Supreme Court decision that by a five-to-four vote struck down a Washington state initiative forbidding busing for racial integration (which had been mandated by a Seattle school board) while allowing it for nonracial purposes. *Washington* v. *Seattle School District No. 1* concerned minorities and not also women, so its relevance is partly in doubt. But the fundamental problem with the argument drawn from the case lies in the assumption that preferences in public employment, education, and contracting, like busing, really do indeed "inure to the benefit" of minorities and women. This was one of the issues bound up in the debate over Proposition 209, and it is not obvious why minorities and women would vote for a measure that is said to be against their interests—unless they disagreed with that. Exit polls showed that 27 percent of blacks, 34 percent of Latinos, and 44 percent of Asians voted for the measure; so did 52 percent of women, and 58 percent of white women—the same as for white men. "It would be the height of arrogance," writes Jeffrey Rosen in *The New Republic*, "for a federal judge, under the guise of protecting 'political participation,' to constitutionalize the policy judgment that the citizens of California rejected: namely, that affirmative action is good for women and minorities."[1] The current Supreme Court would be unlikely to engage in such a display of arrogance, especially since it has said that under the Constitution so-called benign racial classifications deserve just as much judicial skepticism as the bad ones in which harm against minorities is intended.

Late in 1996, Thelton Henderson, the district judge handling the case, temporarily halted the implementation of Proposition 209, expressing his support for the political-participation argument. Given the possibility of additional Clinton appointees to the Ninth Circuit and the Supreme Court, it would be rash to predict how the courts will ultimately treat Proposition 209—a story that will be played out over 1997 and 1998. If Proposition 209 is finally deemed unconstitutional, such a ruling could substantially impede the effort to end public-sector preferences that is now moving east from California. On the other hand, if Proposition 209 is judged constitutional, that decision would quicken the movement and probably hasten the elimination of public-sector preferences.

Proposition 209 already has made history by making the morality and wisdom of preferential treatment a subject of open public debate and decision, for the first time since the advent 30 years ago of affirmative action. The preferential policies begun in the latter half of the 1960s that targeted first blacks and then other racial and ethnic groups, and finally women, were largely hatched in the bureaucracies of government and education, and in the boardrooms of foundations and corporations. Requiring suspension of color-blind principles that had so recently won public approval, these policies were not submitted to the people for their consideration. Nor have their supporters ever wanted such public scrutiny, for obvious reason: Twenty years of surveys had consistently indicated that a majority of Americans oppose preferences. By explicitly proposing to eliminate "preferential treatment," Proposition 209 asked the voters of one of nation's most politically important states to decide whether the public sector should abide by a law that requires no discrimination either for or against someone on grounds of race or sex.

Opponents of Proposition 209 had difficulty arguing against preferential treatment. One tack was to try to deny it even existed in California—a claim belied by much evidence, most notably the admissions policies of the University of California system, which detailed the degree of preference extended in the admissions process to members of certain racial and ethnic groups. Another line of attack was to say that "preferential treatment" doesn't have a legal definition and therefore would be subject to unknown judicial interpretation. "A big, amorphous blob" is what one opponent called preferential treatment. But the term is indeed found in the law—specifically in the 1964 Civil Rights Act and in numerous Supreme Court opinions. And whether for or against it, the authors of those opinions were not perplexed about its meaning—discrimination in favor of someone on account of race or sex.

Opponents also tried to turn Proposition 209 into a vote on "affirmative action," a term that encompasses both preferential and non-preferential procedures and which, precisely because of its ambiguity, enjoys far more public support than does preferential treatment. Over the years, for this reason, supporters of preferences have preferred to talk about affirmative action. But this time they ran into a problem—the fact that the initiative nowhere mentioned "affirmative action." Turning to the California courts, the opponents sought a ruling that would have rewritten the ballot "title and summary" to omit reference to preferential treatment and reflect the initiative's "chief purpose"—"to prohibit affirmative action programs by public entities that are inconsistent with the prohibition in this measure." With the California courts correctly refusing to edit the ballot title and summary, opponents were unable to obscure—as they had so successfully in years past—the issue of preferential treatment.

In the debate reported by and carried out in the news media, Proposition 209 forced consideration of the kind of rule that should apply to government. The race-blind rule that the measure proposed was debated in many quarters precisely as it should have been: in terms of whether or not there might be some circumstances in which race should be a factor in the assignment of public benefits, and in terms of whether, even if there are such circumstances, we are better off with a rule forbidding preferences. Weighed in the balance with this rule was the alternative—the perpetuation of policies that few public officials in California had shown much willingness to mend, much less to end. Indeed, experience over many years in California had taught that state and local preferences when left unchallenged had tended to become permanent.

Finally, Proposition 209 also directed attention to the question of how equal opportunity might be more effectively pursued, without reliance on preferences. Over the years, this question has drawn some interest across the nation, but because of the perdurance of preferences, it has never attracted the discussion it should. Like a hanging, the

prospect of ending preferential treatment focused minds in
California on this question as never before. This will be the
central question facing us as preferential affirmative action is
ended.

Barring the substitution of the judges' will for that of the
people in California, the popular effort to end preferences in
the public sector will continue. But the question remains as
to the relationship of the two major parties to this movement.

The Republican Party remains officially against preferences, but as in previous election years, in 1996 most Republican strategists regarded the issue not as a matter of fundamental principle but merely as a way to move Democratic
voters to the Republican column. Tellingly, when the national
and the state Republican parties finally decided to run television ads in behalf of Proposition 209—they appeared in the
final weeks of the campaign—they did so only because they
thought the ads might produce a larger conservative voter
turnout and thus benefit Dole and other GOP candidates.
The TV ads did not make a case for the initiative but instead
told viewers merely that Clinton was against it. These ads also
clumsily tied Proposition 209 to Proposition 187, the initiative passed in 1994 that ended public benefits for illegal
aliens and which drew strong objections from Hispanic and
Asian voters.

The Republicans' ham-fisted attempt to exploit Proposition 209 backfired even on its own terms, as the GOP lost
congressional seats and control of the state assembly. It also
alienated Democratic voters otherwise inclined to vote for
the measure, which for months had been leading by 20 percentage points in opinion surveys. The authors of the initiative, Glynn Custred and Tom Wood, as well as its chairman,
Ward Connerly, believe they were doing well enough without
the last-hour interventions of their "friends." They believe

that if the Republicans had not decided to campaign for Proposition 209, the measure would have attracted at least 60 percent of the vote, and they may be right.

Until the leadership of the Republican Party regards preferential affirmative action as the serious issue it is, and is willing to debate it year-in and year-out in principled terms that appeal to Americans of all races and ethnic backgrounds, the party will continue to pose more of a hindrance than a help to the effort to end preferences.

As for the Democrats, they remain the party of preferences, notwithstanding the hope of the Democratic Leadership Council in 1992 that Bill Clinton, a "New Democrat," would use the Oval Office to redirect the party toward the principles it once embraced—of individual rights and equality before the law. Worse, the Democratic Party has become the political home of individuals who believe that white people are hopelessly racist, that colorblind laws like CCRI will only ensure white domination over "people of color," and that any person of color who thinks otherwise, who dares embrace individual rights and equality before the law, is "a traitor to his race" or not "authentically" black or Latino or Asian. (Ward Connerly, who is black, was called by California Democrats an Uncle Tom, an "oreo," and worse.) Such beliefs are corrosive to our national unity and lead inexorably to division and distrust.

The Democrats will not soon, or with ease, change direction. But the Democrats' problem is also America's problem, because the ideas that undergird identity politics are being cultivated in universities and law schools and thus are being transmitted to rising generations of young people. At stake is not simply the outcome of this vote or that on preferences but the very possibility of rational conversation about race among all Americans. Whatever President Clinton decides to do on affirmative action during his second term, he would serve the country well by confronting not only instances of racist behavior—that is expected of a president—but also the preachments and practices of racial essentialists.

The most compelling law for a people of all races and ethnic backgrounds remains colorblind law—law that does not allow for discrimination in favor of or against a person on account of race or ethnic background. This understanding, which has a distinguished pedigree in American history and was sincerely held by those advocating civil rights for blacks during the era of segregation, continues to resonate with most Americans. That is why, though there are obstacles political and ideological in the way, and perhaps even a major judicial one, Americans must continue the task, bit by bit if not chunks at a time, of ending preferential affirmative action.

January 1997

Notes

Note: Quotes besides those cited in the text itself or in the following endnotes are from interviews with the author.

Chapter 1. By Any Other Name

1. In December 1995, all five cases were still in litigation.
2. *Hirabayashi* v. *United States,* 320 U.S. 81 (1943).
3. Andrew Kull, *The Color-Blind Constitution* (Cambridge, Mass.: Harvard University Press, 1992), p. 182.
4. 438 U.S. 265 (1978).
5. Alfred W. Blumrosen, *Black Employment and the Law* (New Brunswick, N.J.: Rutgers University Press, 1971), p. viii.
6. See George LaNoue, "Presumptions for Preferences: The Small Business Administration's Decisions on Groups Entitled to Affirmative Action," *Journal of Policy History* 6, no. 4 (1994).
7. Lino A. Graglia, "*Hopwood* v. *Texas:* Racial Preferences in Higher Education Upheld and Endorsed," *Journal of Legal Education* 45, no. 1 (March 1995): 82.

8. "Suit Against U. of Texas Challenges Law School's Affirmative-Action Effort," *Chronicle of Higher Education,* February 9, 1994. Hopwood and three other applicants rejected by the law school filed the lawsuit. See the discussion of the case in chapter 4.

9. Sonia L. Nazario, "Many Minorities Feel Torn by Experience of Affirmative Action," *Wall Street Journal,* June 27, 1989.

10. The letter is quoted in the district court's opinion in *United States v. Board of Education, Township of Piscataway,* 832 F. Supp. 836 (D.N.J. 1994). The court sided with Taxman. The school board has appealed the decision to the Third Circuit Court of Appeals. See the discussion of the case in chapter 5.

11. *Aiken v. City of Memphis,* 37 F. 3d. 1155 (6th Cir. 1994).

12. Phyllis Berman and Alexander Alger, with Toddi Gutner Block, "The Set-Aside Charade," *Forbes,* March 13, 1995.

13. Peter Skerry, "Borders and Quotas: Immigration and the Affirmative-Action State," *The Public Interest,* no. 96 (summer 1989): 93.

14. Jonathan Tilove, "Affirmative Action Has Drawbacks for Blacks," *Cleveland Plain Dealer,* July 20, 1995.

15. 115 S.Ct. 2097 (1995). See the discussion of the case in chapter 6.

Chapter 2. The Fight for Colorblind Law

1. William M. Wiecek, *The Sources of Anti-Slavery Constitutionalism in America, 1760–1848* (Ithaca, N.Y.: Cornell University Press, 1977), pp. 41–42.

2. *Scott v. Sanford,* 60 U.S. 393 (1857). The Lincoln quote is found in Roy P. Basler, ed., *The Collected Works of Abraham Lincoln* (New Brunswick, N.J.: Rutgers University Press, 1953), vol. 3, p. 220.

3. Basler, *Collected Works of Abraham Lincoln,* vol. 2, p. 532.

4. Andrew Kull, *The Color-Blind Constitution* (Cambridge, Mass.: Harvard University Press, 1992), pp. 22–39. Kull's excellent book, on which I rely substantially in this chapter, provides the best account we have of the history of colorblind law.

5. Counsel Charles Sumner's oral argument in *Roberts v. Boston,* in Albert P. Blaustein and Robert L. Zangrando, eds., *Civil Rights and the Black American: A Documentary History* (New York: Washington Square Press, 1970), pp. 114–15.

6. See Kull, *Color-Blind Constitution*, p. 35.

7. Ibid., p. 58.

8. 163 U.S. 537 (1896).

9. See Kull, *Color-Blind Constitution*, pp. 123–24.

10. A. Philip Randolph, "Why Should We March?" in John Hope Franklin and Isidore Starr, eds., *The Negro in Twentieth Century America* (New York: Vintage Books, 1967), pp. 138–40.

11. 320 U.S. 81 (1943); 323 U.S. 214 (1944).

12. 332 U.S. 631 (1948).

13. 339 U.S. 637 (1950).

14. 339 U.S. 629 (1950).

15. Quoted in Richard Kluger, *Simple Justice* (New York: Vintage Books, 1975), pp. 275–76.

16. *Henderson* v. *United States,* 339 U.S. 816 (1950).

17. 347 U.S. 483 (1954).

18. NAACP Brief in *Brown* v. *Board of Education,* in Blaustein and Zangrando, eds., *Civil Rights and the Black American,* pp. 420–21, 423.

19. Shelby Steele, *The Content of Our Character* (New York: St. Martin's Press, 1990), p. 18.

20. Nathan Glazer, *Affirmative Discrimination: Ethnic Inequality and Public Policy* (New York: Basic Books, 1975), p. 43.

21. Hugh Davis Graham, *The Civil Rights Era: Origins and Development of National Policy* (New York: Oxford University Press, 1990), p. 150.

22. Kull, *Color-Blind Constitution*, p. 7.

23. William W. Van Alstyne, "Affirmative Action and Racial Discrimination Under Law: A Preliminary Review," Selected Affirmative Action Topics in Employment and Business Set-Asides, U.S. Commission on Civil Rights, 1985, p. 181.

Chapter 3. Shackled Runners: The Rise of Affirmative Action

1. See *United States* v. *Jefferson County Board of Education,* 372 F.2d 836 (5th Cir. 1966).

2. See Andrew Kull, *The Color-Blind Constitution* (Cambridge, Mass.: Harvard University Press, 1992), p. 166.

3. 402 U.S. 1 (1971).

4. The American Enterprise Institute, "A Conversation with the Rev. Jesse Jackson: The Quest for Economic and Educational Parity," *AEI Studies* 209 (1978): 4.

5. Hugh Davis Graham, *The Civil Rights Era: Origins and Development of National Policy, 1960–1972* (New York: Oxford University Press, 1990), pp. 104–9.

6. Ibid., pp. 111–12.

7. See Charles Murray, *Losing Ground: American Social Policy, 1950–1980* (New York: Basic Books, 1995), p. 44.

8. "Report of the National Advisory Commission on Civil Disorders" in Albert P. Blaustein and Robert L. Zangrando, eds., *Civil Rights and the Black American: A Documentary History* (New York: Washington Square Press, 1968), p. 619.

9. Alfred W. Blumrosen, *Black Employment and the Law* (New Brunswick, N.J.: Rutgers University Press, 1971), p. vii.

10. Graham, *Civil Rights Era*, p. 195.

11. Ibid., p. 286.

12. Ibid., p. 290.

13. Ibid., p. 331.

14. Ibid., p. 334.

15. *Contractors Association of Eastern Pennsylvania* v. *Secretary of Labor*, 311 F. Supp. 1002 (E.D. Pa. 1970).

16. Graham, *Civil Rights Era*, pp. 326–27.

17. 401 U.S. 424 (1971). Justice Blackmun did not participate in the case.

18. Herbert S. Parmet, *Richard Nixon's America* (New York: Little, Brown, 1990), p. 598.

19. See George LaNoue, "Presumptions for Preferences: The Small Business Administration's Decisions on Groups Entitled to Affirmative Action," *Journal of Policy History* 6, no. 4 (1994): 440–41.

20. Herbert Hammerman, "Affirmative-Action Stalemate: A Second Perspective," *The Public Interest*, no. 93 (fall 1988): 131.

21. See the statement of the Harvard College admissions plan, appended to Justice Powell's opinion in *Regents of the University of California* v. *Bakke*, 438 U.S. 265 (1978).

22. McGeorge Bundy, "The Issue Before the Courts: Who Gets Ahead in America," *Atlantic Monthly*, November 1977, p. 54.

23. 438 U.S. 265 (1978).

24. Laurence Silberman, "The Road to Quotas," *Wall Street Journal*, August 11, 1977.

25. 443 U.S. 193 (1979).

26. 448 U.S. 448 (1980).

27. See Thomas Byrne Edsall and Mary D. Edsall, *Chain Reaction: The Impact of Race, Rights, and Taxes on American Politics* (New York: Norton, 1992), pp. 142–43.

Chapter 4. Remediation and Diversity: Affirmative Action in Higher Education

1. 438 U.S. 265 (1978).

2. *Hopwood* v. *Texas*, 861 F.Supp. 551 (W.D. Tex. 1994).

3. Scott Jaschik, "U.S. Judge Upholds Use of Race in Admissions, but Outlines Some Limits," *Chronicle of Higher Education*, September 7, 1994.

4. Shelby Steele, *The Content of Our Character* (New York: St. Martin's Press, 1990), p. 117.

5. The four justices who voted to uphold the Davis program agreed with the conclusion drawn by the medical school. "The failure of minorities to qualify for admission at Davis under regular procedures were due principally to the effects of past discrimination."

6. See Thomas Sowell, *Preferential Policies: An International Perspective* (New York: Little, Brown, 1991), pp. 128–34.

7. Using a composite score made up of a student's LSAT score and undergraduate Grade Point Average (GPA), the school placed applicants into one of three categories: presumptive admit, presumptive reject, and a discretionary zone in between. In 1992, the year Hopwood applied, the presumptive admit score for "whites and others" was 199 and the presumptive reject score was 192. The presumptive admit score for blacks and Mexican-Americans was 189—three points below the presumptive reject score for whites and others.

8. *Podberesky* v. *Kirwan,* 38 F.3d 147 (4th Cir. 1994).

9. Dale Russakoff, "Rutgers Proud of Law-School Set-Asides," *Washington Post,* April 10, 1995.

10. The Diversity Project (Final Report), conducted by the Institute for the Study of Social Change and published by the University of California at Berkeley, November 1991, pp. 23, 28, 32. (Emphasis in the original.)

11. "Re: *Adarand,*" Memorandum to General Counsels from the Office of Legal Counsel, Department of Justice, June 28, 1995.

12. Sowell, *Preferential Policies,* p. 129. As for Justice Powell, he did not use the language of proportional representation, perhaps because he had rejected the remedial rationale and its claim that educational outcomes are a consequence of discrimination. Powell referred readers to the summary of the Harvard College program for guidance on how a school might take race into account. The summary recommends against admitting a token number of students, but then turns vague, advising only that a school would have to pay "some attention to numbers."

13. In its May/June 1995 edition, *Texas Alcalde* raised the problem of racial classification by noting that "even now, students often come from mixed family backgrounds." On this point, the publication quoted from a letter to the school newspaper by a graduate student in education: "What do we tell the mulatto who applies for admission to the University. Does he mark the space in front of the word 'white' or the space in front of the word 'black'? Does he sympathize primarily with his black father who was shut out of the University 40 years ago or with his white mother who was doing the shutting out? How long will we continue to categorize ourselves by race?"

14. Harold Orlans, "Affirmative Action in Higher Education," in "Affirmative Action Revisited," *Annals of the American Academy of Political and Social Science* 523 (September 1992): 147.

15. Peter Applebome, "Gains in Diversity Face Attack in California," *New York Times,* June 4, 1995.

16. *Texas Alcalde* (May/June 1995): 14–15.

17. Yolanda Cruz, "A Twofer's Lament," *The New Republic,* October 17, 1994.

18. Glenn C. Loury, *One by One from the Inside Out: Essays and Reviews on Race and Responsibility in America* (New York: Free Press, 1995), p. 112.

19. The Diversity Project, p. 52.

20. Ibid.

21. In their seminal study of racial politics, Paul M. Sniderman and Thomas Piazza show that "a number of whites dislike the idea of affirmative action so much and perceive it to be so unfair that they have come to dislike blacks as a consequence." For this reason, they write: "In the very effort to make things better, we have made some things worse. Strong arguments can be made in behalf of affirmative action, but its political price must also be recognized. Wishing to close the racial divide in America, we have widened it." Sniderman and Piazza, *The Scar of Race* (Cambridge, Mass.: Harvard University Press, 1993), p. 8.

22. See Glenn C. Loury, "Not-So Black and White: The Two Americas Are Actually Converging," *Washington Post,* October 15, 1995.

23. This information is taken from an article by three political scientists involved in the graduate admissions process at Harvard's government department. The article describes the admissions process in detail and is by no means critical of affirmative action. The authors write: "According to departmental custom, we admit, in a separate affirmative action category, any minority applicant who we believe would complete the program if admitted. . . . If we applied this same rule we are required to use for our Affirmative Action list (admitting those we think would graduate) to all applicants, we would admit 200–300 each year. . . . All minorities receive our maximum financial aid package regardless of need." Note 5 says that "the financial aid package for minorities is more lucrative than that for all non-minority admits." Gary King, John M. Bruce, Michael Gilligan, "The Science of Political Science Graduate Admissions," *PS: Political Science and Politics* (December 1993): 772–78.

Chapter 5. Counting and Norming:
Affirmative Action in the Workplace

1. Businesses with fewer than fifteen employees are exempt from Title VII. The figures in this paragraph are based on government data reported in "Reforming Affirmative Action in Employment: How to Restore the Law of Equal Treatment" by Nelson Lund, a paper published by the Heritage Foundation in Washington, D.C., August 2, 1995, p. 3.

2. 443 U.S. 193 (1979).

3. The emphasis is in the Court's opinion.

4. Quoted in Herman Belz, *Equality Transformed: A Quarter Century of Affirmative Action* (New Brunswick, N.J.: Transaction Press, 1992), p. 160.

5. In early 1981, the Justice Department announced that it would pursue nonquota remedies in cases of proven discrimination on the part of public employers. In 1985, the EEOC, which enforces Title VII in the private sector, decided to follow the same policy. During the 1970s, the Supreme Court had not ruled on the validity of judicially ordered numerical remedies. In the 1984 case of *Firefighters* v. *Stotts*, the Justice Department persuaded the Court that federal judges lack authority under Title VII to impose race-based layoffs upon an employer found in violation of the law. But the department failed in its effort to use the *Stotts* decision to eliminate court-ordered quotas for hiring and promoting minorities and women.

6. Belz, *Equality Transformed*, p. 195. See also Gary L. McDowell, "Affirmative Inaction," *Policy Review*, no. 48 (spring 1989): 32–37.

7. Anne B. Fisher, "Businessmen Like to Hire by the Numbers," *Fortune*, September 16, 1985, p. 27.

8. 480 U.S. 616 (1987).

9. There was no question here of Labor Department pressure to hire by the numbers, for the agency was a public employer. And unlike Kaiser Aluminum, the agency did not fear a Title VII lawsuit based on low numbers of minorities or women employed in certain job categories. Thus the agency had not drawn up its

affirmative action plan in response to that part of the proquota legal environment that affected public employers. Instead, the agency had devised its plan because it believed—or at least its leadership believed—in numerical affirmative action.

10. Belz, *Equality Transformed*, p. 225.

11. 109 S.Ct. 2115 (1989).

12. Alfred W. Blumrosen, *Black Employment and the Law* (New Brunswick, N.J.: Rutgers University Press, 1971), p. viii.

13. Peter Applebome, "Class Notes," *New York Times*, May 17, 1995.

14. *United States* v. *Board of Education, Township of Piscataway*, 832 F.Supp. 836 (D.N.J. 1994).

15. Alfred W. Blumrosen, "How the Courts Are Handling Reverse Discrimination Claims," *Daily Labor Report*, March 23, 1995.

16. One reason the extent of preferential treatment is unknown is that it is very hard to separate the effects of preferential affirmative action in the workplace from broader civil rights enforcement. Some economists contend that the Labor Department's enforcement of affirmative action has mainly shifted minorities from firms that do not contract with the government to those that do. See Farrell Bloch, *Antidiscrimination Law and Minority Employment* (Chicago: University of Chicago Press, 1994), and Dave M. O'Neill and June O'Neill, "Affirmative Action in the Labor Market," in "Affirmative Action Revisited," *Annals of the American Academy of Political and Social Science* 523 (September 1992): 88–103.

Chapter 6. Stacking the Deck:
Affirmative Action in Contracting

1. Andrea Stone, "The Other Side of Quotas," *USA Today*, July 19, 1995.

2. "Procurements in the Telecommunications Services Resale Market," Report No. 95–159, Office of the Inspector General, Department of Defense, April 5, 1995.

3. 448 U.S. 448.

4. Andrew Kull, *The Color-Blind Constitution* (Cambridge, Mass.: Harvard University Press, 1992), p. 208, note 71.

5. 488 U.S. 469.

6. Evidence in the case showed that MBEs in Richmond received a higher percentage than this of all public contracts—between 7 and 8 percent.

7. Terry Eastland, "Racial Preferences in Court—Again," *Commentary* (January 1989).

8. The 1980 census for Richmond (population 219,214) counted 2,210 persons of Spanish origin, 75 of Japanese, 264 of Chinese, 81 of Filipino, 146 of Korean, 226 of Vietnamese, 34 of Hawaiian, 9 of Samoan, and 139 of Asian Indian. Also, it reported 781 in the "other" category. There were three Eskimos and two Aleuts. These groups amounted to 1.82 percent, while Richmond's 112,357 blacks accounted for 51.3 percent.

9. 497 U.S. 547 (1990).

10. 115 S.Ct. 2097 (1995).

11. *Cornelius* v. *Los Angeles Metropolitan Transportation Authority*, July 27, 1995.

12. Here again it must be noted that the attempt to infer discrimination from a disparity, no matter how finely it is drawn, is dubious: many variables, including the size and experience of a business, may explain why it wins or loses a government contract. Assuming the availability of the necessary data, which very few jurisdictions have, the most plausible disparity study would be a multiple regression analysis, which seeks to determine the effect of a particular variable while holding all others constant. See John Lunn, "Markets, Discrimination, and Affirmative Action: Economic Theory and Evidence," in *Racial Preferences in Government Contracting*, ed. Roger Clegg (Washington, D.C.: National Legal Center for the Public Interest, 1993), pp. 59–60.

13. Testimony of George R. LaNoue, Joint Hearings of the Subcommittee on the Constitution, Federalism, and Property of the Senate Judiciary Committee and the Subcommittee on the Constitution of the House Judiciary Committee, September 22, 1995.

14. See *Bras* v. *California Public Utilities Commission*, No. 93-15764, Ninth Circuit Court of Appeals, July 5, 1995.

15. George R. LaNoue, "The Disparity Study Shield: Baltimore and San Francisco," in Clegg, ed., *Racial Preferences in Government Contracting*, p. 72, note 14.

16. Paul M. Barrett and Michael K. Frisby, "Affirmative-Action Advocates Seeking Lessons from States to Help Preserve Federal Programs," *Wall Street Journal*, June 14, 1995.

17. George R. LaNoue, "The Demographic Premises of Affirmative Action," *Population and Environment: A Journal of Interdisciplinary Studies* 14, no. 5 (May 1993): 436–37.

18. Thomas W. Lippman, "Energizing Minorities' Objectives," *Washington Post*, December 1, 1992.

19. Stephanie N. Mehta, "Affirmative-Action Supporters Face Divisive Problem," *Wall Street Journal*, June 2, 1995.

20. Jeff Rosen, "The Colorblind Court," *The New Republic*, July 31, 1995.

Chapter 7. The Immigration Factor

1. Deroy Murdock, "Time to Set Aside All Set-Asides," *New York Post*, February 14, 1994.

2. Lawrence H. Fuchs, *The American Kaleidoscope: Race, Ethnicity, and the Civic Culture* (Hanover, N.H.: Wesleyan University Press, 1995), p. xix.

3. Lawrence H. Fuchs, "What Do Immigrants Deserve?" *Washington Post*, January 24, 1995.

4. George R. LaNoue, "Presumptions for Preferences: The Small Business Administration's Decisions on Groups Entitled to Affirmative Action," *Journal of Policy History* 6, no. 4 (1994): 439–67.

5. James S. Robb, *Affirmative Action for Immigrants: The Entitlement Nobody Wanted* (Petoskey, Mich.: The Social Contract Press, 1995), pp. 99–101.

6. Peter Skerry, "Borders and Quotas: Immigration and the Affirmative-Action State," *The Public Interest*, no. 96 (summer 1989): 88–89.

7. George R. LaNoue, "The Demographic Premises of Affirmative Action," *Population and Environment* 14, no. 5 (May 1993): 426–27.

8. See Glazer, "Race, Not Class," and Fuchs, *The American Kaleido-scope,* pp. 453–57.

9. The research is summarized in Howard Schuman, Charlotte Steeh, and Lawrence Bobo, *Racial Attitudes in America* (Cambridge, Mass.: Harvard University Press, 1988).

10. William Raspberry, "What Actions Are Affirmative?" *Washington Post,* August 21, 1995.

11. Thus, Randall Kennedy of the Harvard Law School argues that affirmative action should be retained because it is useful in overcoming "entrenched racial hierarchy." See his article "Persuasion and Distrust" in *Racial Preference and Racial Justice: The New Affirmative Action Controversy,* Russell Nieli, ed. (Washington, D.C.: Ethics and Public Policy Center, 1991), pp. 47–48.

12. James Smith and Finis Welch, *Closing the Gap: Forty Years of Economic Progress for Blacks* (Santa Monica, Calif.: The Rand Corporation, 1986).

13. William Julius Wilson, *The Truly Disadvantaged* (Chicago: University of Chicago Press, 1978), pp. 18–19.

14. Nicholas Lemann, "Taking Affirmative Action Apart," *New York Times Magazine,* June 11, 1995, p. 62.

15. The studies are discussed in Nathan Glazer, "The Affirmative Action Stalemate," *The Public Interest,* no. 90 (winter 1988): 110.

16. Paul M. Sniderman and Thomas Piazza, *The Scar of Race* (Cambridge, Mass.: Harvard University Press, 1993), pp. 5, 177.

17. Both studies await publication. They are: "The Politics of Affirmative Action," by James H. Kuklinski, Paul M. Sniderman, Kathleen Knight, Thomas Piazza, Philip E. Tetlock, Gordon R. Lawrence, and Barbara Mellers; and "Affirmative Action and the Politics of Realignment," by Martin Gilens, Paul M. Sniderman, and James H. Kuklinski. The latter study advances the new finding that opposition to affirmative action is "just as prevalent among liberals and Democrats as among conservatives and Republicans." It observes: "Opposition to affirmative action is both pervasive among the white public and broadly spread across the political spectrum because the most important source of this opposition is so broadly distributed among the white public."

18. See Everett Carll Ladd, "Affirmative Action, Welfare, and the Individual," *Public Perspective* 6, no. 4 (June/July 1995).

Chapter 8. The Ground Shifts

1. Seymour Martin Lipset and William Schneider, "The Bakke Case," *Public Opinion,* March/April 1978, pp. 38–44.

2. Seymour Martin Lipset, "Equal Chances Versus Equal Results," in "Affirmative Action Revisited," Harold Orlans and June O'Neill, eds., *Annals of the American Academy of Political and Social Science* (September 1992): 66–69.

3. Everett Carll Ladd, "Affirmative Action, Welfare, and the Individual," *Public Perspective* 6, no. 4 (June/July 1995): 23–24. See also Jack Citrin, "Affirmative Action in the People's Court," *The Public Interest* (winter 1996): 39–48.

4. U.S. Bureau of the Census, 1990 Census of the Population, Supplementary Reports, *Detailed Occupation and Other Characteristics from the EEO File for the United States* (Washington, D.C.: U.S. Government Printing Office, 1992), Table 1.

5. Glynn Custred, "What Went Wrong with Affirmative Action," *Academe,* November/December 1995, p. 12.

6. "Race-Based Admissions at University of California Medical Schools," Pacific Research Institute, San Francisco, Calif., June 1995.

7. *Hayes* v. *North State Law Enforcement Officers Ass'n,* 10 F.3d 207 (4th Cir. 1993).

8. See Jonathan Rauch, "Color TV," *The New Republic,* December 19, 1994, pp. 9–12.

9. "Re: *Adarand,*" Memorandum of the Office of Legal Counsel to Heads of Executive Departments and Agencies, July 5, 1995.

10. D'Vera Cohn, "Ambivalence in Maryland Echoes Across the Nation," *Washington Post,* October 11, 1995.

11. Citrin, "Affirmative Action in the People's Court," pp. 44–45.

12. Will Marshall, "From Preferences to Empowerment: A New Bargain on Affirmative Action," *Progressive Policy Institute Report,* August 3, 1995.

13. "Honeywell Group Keeps Commitment to Affirmative Action Plan," *Daily Labor Report,* August 1, 1995.
14. Dinesh D'Souza, *The End of Racism* (New York: The Free Press, 1995), pp. 544–45.

Chapter 9. Ending Affirmative Action

1. See Lawrence H. Fuchs, *The American Kaleidoscope: Race, Ethnicity, and the Civic Culture* (Hanover, N.H.: Wesleyan University Press, 1995), p. 456.
2. As for whether the Court should declare the Constitution flatly colorblind—a position endorsed by Justices Antonin Scalia and Clarence Thomas—the issue involves complicated and controversial questions, starting with the original meaning of the Fourteenth Amendment. See Jeff Rosen, "The Colorblind Court," *The New Republic,* July 31, 1995, and Andrew Kull, *The Color-Blind Constitution* (Cambridge, Mass.: Harvard University Press, 1992), pp. 221–24.
3. Roy P. Basler, ed., *The Collected Works of Abraham Lincoln* (New Brunswick, N.J.: Rutgers University Press, 1953), vol. 2, pp. 499–500.

Afterword to the Paperback Edition

1. Jeffrey Rosen, "Stare Indecisis," *The New Republic*, December 23, 1996.

Acknowledgments

M_y own research has bene-
fited from the assistance of Marianne Geers, Heidi Metcalf,
Christopher Hickey, and Jennifer Speigel. Those who read
parts or all of the book at various stages include Christopher
Caldwell, Michael Carvin, Roger Clegg, Doug Cox, Brian Jones,
Fred Siegel, Abigail Thernstrom, Stephan Thernstrom, and
Michael Uhlmann. I thank each one for their insightful comments. My agent Rafe Sagalyn did his usual excellent job.
Rafe introduced me to Paul Golob, as fine an editor as anyone could want. Paul helped me at every level of composition, wielding a knowing pencil as the book moved to its final
draft. My wife Jill and my daughter Katie bore with me during those odd hours when the book demanded my attention;
for their patience, but also for their willingness to interrupt
me, I am especially grateful.

Index